Pathological Gambling

Psychological Disorders

Psychological
Disorders

Pathological Gambling

Christine Adamec

Series Editor
M. Foster Olive, Ph.D.
Assistant Professor of Psychology
Arizona State University

Foreword by
Pat Levitt, Ph.D.
Director, Zilkha Neurogenetic Institute
Chair, Department of Cell and Neurobiology
Keck School of Medicine of USC

CHELSEA HOUSE
PUBLISHERS
An imprint of Infobase Publishing

Pathological Gambling

Chelsea House
An imprint of Infobase Publishing
132 West 31st Street
New York NY 10001

Library of Congress Cataloging-in-Publication Data
Adamec, Christine A., 1949-
  Pathological gambling / by Christine Adamec ; foreword by Pat Levitt. — 1st ed.
      p. cm.
  Includes index.
  ISBN-13: 978-1-60413-942-6 (hardcover : alk. paper)
  ISBN-10: 1-60413-942-0 (hardcover : alk. paper) 1. Compulsive gambling. I. Title.

  RC569.5.G35A33 2010
  616.85'227—dc22

                                2010024898

Chelsea House books are available at special discounts when purchased in bulk quantities for businesses, associations, institutions, or sales promotions. Please call our Special Sales Department in New York at (212) 967-8800 or (800) 322-8755.

You can find Chelsea House on the World Wide Web at http://www.chelseahouse.com

Text design by Keith Trego
Cover design by Keith Trego and Alicia Post
Composition by EJB Publishing Services
Cover printed by Bang Printing, Brainerd, MN
Book printed and bound by Bang Printing, Brainerd, MN
Date printed: December 2010
Printed in the United States of America

10 9 8 7 6 5 4 3 2 1

This book is printed on acid-free paper.

All links and Web addresses were checked and verified to be correct at the time of publication. Because of the dynamic nature of the Web, some addresses and links may have changed since publication and may no longer be valid.

Table of Contents

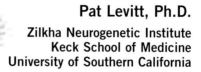

Foreword

Pat Levitt, Ph.D.
Zilkha Neurogenetic Institute
Keck School of Medicine
University of Southern California

Think of the most complicated aspect of our universe, and then multiply that by infinity! Even the most enthusiastic of mathematicians and physicists acknowledge that the brain is by far the most challenging entity to understand. By design, the human brain is made up of billions of cells called neurons, which use chemical neurotransmitters to communicate with each other through connections called synapses. Each brain cell has about 2,000 synapses. Connections between neurons are not formed in a random fashion, but rather are organized into a type of architecture that is far more complex than any of today's supercomputers. And, not only is the brain's connective architecture more complex than any computer; its connections are capable of *changing* to improve the way a circuit functions. For example, the way we learn new information involves changes in circuits that actually improve performance. Yet some change can also result in a disruption of connections, like changes that occur in disorders such as drug addiction, depression, schizophrenia, and epilepsy, or even changes that can increase a person's risk of suicide.

Genes and the environment are powerful forces in building the brain during development and ensuring normal brain functioning, but they can also be the root causes of psychological and neurological disorders when things go awry. The way in which brain architecture is built before birth and in childhood will determine how well the brain functions when we are adults, and even how susceptible we are to such diseases as depression, anxiety, or attention disorders, which can severely disturb brain function. In a sense, then, understanding how the brain is built can lead us to a clearer picture of the ways in which our brain works, how we can improve its functioning, and what we can do to repair it when diseases strike.

Brain architecture reflects the highly specialized jobs that are performed by human beings, such as seeing, hearing, feeling, smelling, and moving. Different brain areas are specialized to control specific functions. Each specialized area must communicate well with other areas for the brain to accomplish even more complex tasks, like controlling body physiology—our patterns of sleep, for example, or even our eating habits, both of which can become disrupted if brain development or function is disturbed in some way. The brain controls our feelings, fears, and emotions; our ability to learn and store new information; and how well we recall old information. The brain does all this, and more, by building, during development, the circuits that control these functions, much like a hard-wired computer. Even small abnormalities that occur during early brain development through gene mutations, viral infection, or fetal exposure to alcohol can increase the risk of developing a wide range of psychological disorders later in life.

Those who study the relationship between brain architecture and function, and the diseases that affect this bond, are neuroscientists. Those who study and treat the disorders that are caused by changes in brain architecture and chemistry are psychiatrists and psychologists. Over the last 50 years, we have learned quite a lot about how brain architecture and chemistry work and how genetics contributes to brain structure and function. Genes are very important in controlling the initial phases of building the brain. In fact, almost every gene in the human genome is needed to build the brain. This process of brain development actually starts prior to birth, with almost all the neurons we will ever have in our brain produced by mid-gestation. The assembly of the architecture, in the form of intricate circuits, begins by this time, and by birth we have the basic organization laid out. But the work is not yet complete because billions of connections form over a remarkably long period of time, extending through puberty. The brain of a child is being built and modified on a daily basis, even during sleep.

While there are thousands of chemical building blocks, such as proteins, lipids, and carbohydrates, that are used much like bricks and mortar to put the architecture together, the highly detailed connectivity that emerges during childhood depends greatly upon experiences and our environment. In building a house, we use specific blueprints to assemble the basic structures, like a foundation, walls, floors, and ceilings. The brain is assembled similarly. Plumbing and electricity, like the basic circuitry of the brain, are put in place early in the building process. But for all of this early work, there is another very important phase of development, which is termed experience-dependent development. During the first three years of life, our brains actually form far more connections than we will ever need, almost 40 percent more! Why would this occur? Well, in fact, the early circuits form in this way so that we can use experience to mold our brain architecture to best suit the functions that we are likely to need for the rest of our lives

Experience is not just important for the circuits that control our senses. A young child who experiences toxic stress, like physical abuse, will have his or her brain architecture changed in regions that will result in poorer control of emotions and feelings as an adult. Experience is powerful. When we repeatedly practice on the piano or shoot a basketball hundreds of times daily, we are using experience to model our brain connections to function at their finest. Some will achieve better results than others, perhaps because the initial phases of circuit-building provided a better base, just like the architecture of houses may differ in terms of their functionality. We are working to understand the brain structure and function that result from the powerful combination of genes building the initial architecture and a child's experience adding the all-important detailed touches. We also know that, like an old home, the architecture can break down. The aging process can be particularly hard on the ability of brain circuits to function at their best because positive change comes less readily as we get older. Synapses may be lost and brain chemistry can change over time. The difficulties in understanding how architecture gets built are paralleled by the complexities of what happens to that architecture as we grow older. Dementia associated with brain deterioration as a complication of Alzheimer's disease and memory loss associated with aging or alcoholism are active avenues of research in the neuroscience community.

There is truth, both for development and in aging, in the old adage "use it or lose it." Neuroscientists are pursuing the idea that brain architecture and chemistry can be modified well beyond childhood. If we understand the mechanisms that make it easy for a young, healthy brain to learn or repair itself following an accident, perhaps we can use those same tools to optimize the functioning of aging brains. We already know many ways in which we can improve the functioning of the aging or injured brain. For example, for an individual who has suffered a stroke that has caused structural damage to brain architecture, physical exercise can be quite powerful in helping to reorganize circuits so that they function better, even in an elderly individual. And you know that when you exercise and sleep regularly, you just feel better. Your brain chemistry and architecture are functioning at their best. Another example of ways we can improve nervous system function are the drugs that are used to treat mental illnesses. These drugs are designed to change brain chemistry so that the neurotransmitters used for communication between brain cells can function more normally. These same types of drugs, however, when taken in excess or abused, can actually damage brain chemistry and change brain architecture so that it functions more poorly.

As you read the Psychological Disorders series, the images of altered brain organization and chemistry will come to mind in thinking about complex diseases such as schizophrenia or drug addiction. There is nothing more fascinating and important to understand for the well-being of humans. But also keep in mind that as neuroscientists, we are on a mission to comprehend human nature, the way we perceive the world, how we recognize color, why we smile when thinking about the Thanksgiving turkey, the emotion of experiencing our first kiss, or how we can remember the winner of the 1953 World Series. If you are interested in people, and the world in which we live, you are a neuroscientist, too.

Pat Levitt, Ph.D.
Director, Zilkha Neurogenetic Institute
Chair, Department of Cell and Neurobiology
Keck School of Medicine
University of Southern California

An Overview

Darlene, 25, was absolutely certain she could quit gambling anytime that she felt like it—it's just that she never wanted to stop. Her family and friends were very worried about her because all Darlene seemed to care about was going to Atlantic City (about an hour from her home in New York City) to play the slots; she had also maxed out all her credit cards to buy lottery tickets at home. Darlene frequently asked her parents, friends, and others to lend her at least $50 so she could buy some food—yet she was looking increasingly scrawny to everyone, so they began wondering aloud where all the money for the so-called food was really going. Was she maybe on drugs? (She was not.) These "loans" were also never paid back, which nearly everyone had learned by now.

Darlene was a little late on paying the rent again and the landlord was threatening eviction. But she figured he wouldn't actually go through with it, and so she concentrated instead on excitedly planning her next big gambling adventure.

Darlene has a gambling problem. If she were evaluated with the criteria for pathological gambling from the Diagnostic and Statistical Manual (DSM), *published by the American Psychiatric Association,[1] or with the South Oaks Gambling Screen,[2] a popular screening tool used by many experts, she would definitely fulfill the criteria of a pathological gambler.*

Pathological gambling is a serious problem in the United States, as is problem gambling, a term often used to describe the habits of individuals who gamble to excess but do not meet the full criteria for pathological gambling. In 2004, the Department of Justice estimated that about 2.5 million Americans were **pathological gamblers** and 3 million were **problem gamblers**.[3] Others such as Ronald Kessler and colleagues have estimated the numbers of pathological gamblers at less than 1 million.[4] Although experts disagree on the number of pathological gamblers in the United States, they agree that pathological gambling is a serious problem.

Pathological gamblers and problem gamblers are more likely than non-gamblers to have many serious problems in their lives as well as cause major problems in the lives of others; for example, they have an increased risk for going bankrupt, getting divorced, losing their jobs, getting arrested, and suffering many other negative consequences of their **compulsive gambling**.[5] In general, the younger the gambler when he or she first starts gambling, the greater is the risk for the subsequent development of pathological gambling.[6] However, a desire to recover, combined with effective treatment, can help many pathological gamblers turn their lives around, whatever their age.

DETERMINING WHETHER PEOPLE ARE PATHOLOGICAL GAMBLERS

The American Psychiatric Association (APA) categorizes pathological gambling as an **impulse control disorder** and provides specific criteria for pathological gamblers in the *Diagnostic and Statistical Manual Text Revision (DSM-IV-TR)*. The APA criteria are as follows:

A. Persistent and recurrent maladaptive gambling behavior as indicated by five (or more) of the following:
   (1) is preoccupied with gambling (e.g., preoccupied with reliving past gambling experiences, handicapping

Figure 1.1 Lottery tickets are readily purchased in nearly every state. (©*AP Images*)

or planning the next venture, or thinking of ways to get money with which to gamble)

(2) needs to gamble with increasing amounts of money in order to achieve the desired excitement

(3) has repeated unsuccessful efforts to control, cut back, or stop gambling

(4) is restless or irritable when attempting to cut down or stop gambling

(5) gambles as a way of escaping from problems or of relieving a dysphoric mood (e.g., feelings of helplessness, guilt, anxiety, depression)

(6) after losing money gambling, often returns another day to get even ("chasing" one's losses)

(7) lies to family members, therapists or others to conceal the extent of involvement with gambling

(8) has committed illegal acts such as forgery, fraud, theft, or embezzlement to finance gambling

(9) has jeopardized or lost a significant relationship, job, or educational or career opportunity because of gambling

(10) relies on others to provide money to relieve a desperate financial situation caused by gambling

B. The gambling behavior is not better accounted for by a Manic Episode.[7]

(Source: Diagnostic and Statistical Manual of Mental Disorders: DSM-IV-TR. 4th Edition (Paper) by American Psychiatric Association. Copyright 2000 by American Psychiatric Association (DSM). Reproduced with permission of American Psychiatric Assocation (DSM) in the format Tradebook via Copyright Clearance Center.)

A manic episode is a circumstance in which an individual behaves in an extremely hyperactive manner, exhibiting behavior that is not normal for the person. For example, a person with bipolar disorder in the grip of a manic episode might gamble heavily and lose a lot of money, but this behavior is not typical for the individual. In contrast, such behavior is typical for the pathological gambler.

PATHOLOGICAL GAMBLERS AND TERMINOLOGY

The terminology that experts use to describe people with gambling problems can vary considerably. For example, some experts dislike the term "pathological gambling," and so they use "compulsive gambling" instead to describe the same behavior. As mentioned, some experts report on individuals who are "problem gamblers," these being people who meet

Figure 1.2 Casino gambling is available in many states. *(©AP Images)*

fewer *DSM* or other screening criteria for gambling than those with pathological gambling. In addition, some experts use their own particular nomenclature to denote pathological or problem gambling. Some researchers include pathological gamblers and problems gamblers in a single category that they call "**disordered gamblers.**"[8]

In their study on predictive factors for pathological gambling, Renee M. Cunningham-Williams and colleagues use the phrase "sub-threshold gamblers" to describe individuals who have between one and four lifetime *DSM-IV* criteria for pathological gambling, compared to at least five criteria from the *DSM* for those who are pathological gamblers.[9]

Confusingly, some experts use the term "problem gambling" when they really mean "pathological gambling." If a study or book describes out-of-control gambling that is harmful to the person's life, the author is often alluding to pathological gambling.

A Partial List of Types of Gambling Available Today

Bingo and high-stakes bingo

Card games

Casino gambling

Day trading of stocks

Dice games

Greyhound dog racing

Horse racing

Internet gambling

Jai alai

Keno

Lottery tickets

Numbers betting

Office pools

Off-track betting (OTB)

Pull-tabs

Raffles

Riverboat gambling

Roulette

Slot machines

Sports bets

Video-terminal betting

Table 1.1: How the Pathological Gambler Thinks vs. How the Non-Pathological Gambler Thinks

PATHOLOGICAL GAMBLER	NON-PATHOLOGICAL GAMBLER
I just lost! I have to chase my losses by playing more.	I just lost. I had better stop playing.
I ran out of money. I'll see if I can get a loan from someone so I can keep playing.	I ran out of money. I have to stop playing now.
I just won! I'll continue to play and probably win more.	I just won. I'll pocket my winnings and quit while I'm ahead.
I feel lucky, so I'm going to bet everything on "red."	I feel kind of lucky. I'll bet some money and see how I do.
My friends are all having fun betting on whether the team will win. I want to get in the fun too.	My friends are all having fun betting on whether the team will win, but I am all out of money. I better sit this one out.
The rent is due tomorrow, but if I bet and win, then I'll have extra money!	The rent is due tomorrow. I have to hold the rent money aside so I can still pay it if I lose.
Wow, I just got a check that I wasn't expecting! I bet I can double my money—and if I don't, it doesn't matter because this money was a surprise.	Wow, I just got an extra check! I think I'll set aside part of it to splurge and use the rest to pay some bills.
It's raining out and I'm bored. I'll feel a lot better if I go to the casino!	It's raining out and I'm bored. I think I'll call a friend and maybe we can go to the movies or do something else.
I lost last week so that means I'm due for a win this week. I'm ready to gamble.	I lost last week and I could lose again this week. I can't afford to gamble this week.
If I bring my lucky necklace/rabbit's foot/other item, I increase my odds of winning.	Lucky charms or talismans can't make me win. There is no magic involved and it's just chance if I win or lose.

THE MEANS OF GAMBLING USED BY MOST PEOPLE

There are many ways for people to gamble their money, whether they gamble occasionally for fun or they are pathological gamblers who feel compelled to gamble. **Lottery** tickets are readily purchased in nearly every state and there are card games and other games of chance, **casino** gambling, high-stakes bingo, and many other opportunities to gamble in most states in the United States. Some people go on a cruise ship or a riverboat to gamble, while others, like Darlene, particularly enjoy the luxurious ambience of a fancy casino. Others gamble from their homes, using the Internet.

Some people are so addicted to gambling that they will not leave the gaming table or the slot machine that they have been using for hours, even to use the restroom, because they think "What if my table/machine suddenly pays off while I'm gone?" So they risk their health as well as the possibility of an embarrassing personal accident, and instead stay the course. To them, there is no question of acting otherwise.

HOW A PATHOLOGICAL GAMBLER THINKS

Perhaps somewhat surprisingly, experts say that pathological gambling is not usually about winning or even about a desire to attain more money, despite what the gambler tells others or even thinks to himself or herself. Instead, for pathological gamblers, what keeps pulling them back to their gambling venues of choice are the euphoria and the adrenaline rush that come with taking a chance. For pathological gamblers, often it is the gambling itself that can remove them far from life's daily problems, transporting them to a much more exciting world, and one where anything is possible.

Gerda Reith explained this urge as follows:

This uncontrollable desire for excitement and thrills is so overwhelming that even money loses its value in the face of it, becoming devalued to the status of little more than a plaything, a counter in a game (almost literally, in the case of the use of chips in the casino). Although representing the supreme measure of value in the world outside, for problem gamblers, money is simply the medium of play, the price of a good time, or alternately, the cost of an escape from a bad one. Either way, it is dissociated from material consumption and prized not as an end in itself but for its ability to allow continued consumption in repeated play.[10]

Some teenagers are pathological gamblers, and Jeffrey Derevensky and colleagues describe the adolescent gambler in this way (many pathological gamblers could be described similarly):

Through their gambling, adolescents frequently dissociate and escape into another world, often with altered egos and repression of unpleasant daily events or long-term problems. Adolescents with serious gambling problems report that all their problems disappear while they are gambling. They report that betting on the outcome of a sporting event, watching the spinning reels of a video lottery terminal machine or an electronic gaming machine, or scratching an instant lottery ticket provides a rush, increasing their heart rate and intensifying excitement.[11]

It is also the excitement of "not knowing" combined with the possibility of winning that draws pathological and problem gamblers, triggering a state of euphoria. As a result, the higher the gambling odds are and the greater that the risk is, then the bigger the emotional rush. This is why many pathological gamblers reportedly steer away from games of skill, such as poker, and instead they largely gravitate toward games or bets involving pure chance, such as dice or slot machines.

This is also why, whether the pathological gambler wins or loses, he or she *must* return yet again to gambling as soon as possible, in order to duplicate the excitement that gambling invariably generates.[12]

See the table in this chapter, which compares the thinking of the pathological gambler to the thinking in the same situation of the non-pathological gambler. For example, when pathological gamblers lose, they often convince themselves that they need to gamble more to "chase" their previous losses. The non-pathological gambler who gambles may be nonplussed by losing, but he or she usually simply stops gambling.

Gambling and Its History in the United States

Since before 1620, when a lottery funded the historic voyage of the Pilgrims on the *Mayflower* to Plymouth Rock, Massachusetts,[1] gambling has been used to finance many public and private projects and to increase the coffers of many cities and counties. Today, state-run gambling venues in the form of lotteries continue to provide revenues to most states in the United States. Of course, people were gambling, sometimes excessively, well before the Pilgrims set off for the New World. For example, historians report that thousands of years ago, heavy gamblers who ran out of money and property but still wanted to continue their gambling would sell themselves to others as slaves.[2] The definition of pathological gambling was not introduced until the late twentieth century by the American Psychiatric Association, but certainly selling oneself into slavery qualifies as behavior indicating likely pathological gambling.

GAMBLING FROM THE EIGHTEENTH TO THE NINETEENTH CENTURY

A cyclical sentiment for and against gambling ventures in society has been a pattern in the United States since the colonial era of our nation's history; for example, in the colonial era, the colonies used lotteries to generate money for highways, bridges, dams, and all sorts of public works. As stated by

Vicki Abt and coauthors, "This method of public finance was continued by the States following 1776 in the form of State-franchised private lottery companies, and their success in generating revenues is convincing evidence that gambling, at least at lotteries, enjoyed a considerable measure of social approval regardless of its legal status."[3]

Riverboat Gambling

Riverboat gambling became popular starting in 1812 with the steamboat *New Orleans*. In the cities of New Orleans and other towns along the Missouri, Arkansas, Illinois, and Ohio rivers, goods were transported by riverboat and gambling was also offered. By 1860, more than 700 steamboats offered gambling.[5] Cards and dice were easily transportable and "card sharps" (cheaters) were a constant presence on riverboats.

But gambling did not remain accepted by society. In the Southeast in the 1880s, gambling towns began to struggle to attain respectability, the presence of professional gamblers was deemed unacceptable, and some professional gamblers were run out of town or even lynched. By the end of the nineteenth

A Presidential Gambler

Andrew Jackson, the nation's seventh president (1829–1837), was an inveterate gambler, and he once killed a man (and nearly died himself) in a duel that was fought in 1805 over the terms of a bet on a horse race, a race which was never actually run. Jackson had previously lost two fortunes from gambling debts. It is likely that Jackson was a pathological gambler, although the term did not exist in his era and in fact, gambling held a certain respectability in his time.[4]

Figure 2.1 Gamblers in Las Vegas, 1935. *(© Corbis)*

century in the United States, the heyday of riverboat gambling was essentially over.[6] According to Abt et al., by 1900, anti-gambling statutes were present in state constitutions.[7]

THE TWENTIETH CENTURY

Sentiment shifted again after the Great Depression, when states began to realize that rather than having to raise state and local taxes, income could be generated through gambling. The state of Nevada legalized gambling in 1931, and during the next 10 years, pari-mutuel betting on horses was legalized in many Eastern states.[8]

The Rise of "Sin City": Las Vegas, Nevada, and Gambling

In the early days of legalized gambling in Las Vegas, the city was dominated by gambling parlors with a Wild West theme and a small-town atmosphere. None of the glitz, sparkle, and flashing neon lights associated with today's Las Vegas was present when gambling first became legal in Nevada. Nevada was also seen as a good place for a quickie divorce: Divorces were granted after only a six-week residency, in contrast to many states that required (as many still do) residency for at least six months to a year before a person could obtain a divorce in the state's court. This was a purposeful choice made by the state legislature to attract divorcing people to Nevada, although gambling attracted some people. But many moneyed people did their gambling in Cuba and other international locations.

The success of Las Vegas as a glamorous gambling location largely started with mobster Benjamin "Bugsy" Siegel, who took over a gambling location from another man with a dream but without the money to finance it. Taking over the project, Siegel financed it with mobster money, spending lavishly, expending an estimated $7 million, grossly overrunning the $1 million budget on his casino, the Flamingo.

The casino did not immediately succeed when it opened because the hotel was not completed and the weather was bad. The operation was initially considered a flop, so the Flamingo was closed, reopening a few months later in March 1947. Siegel was subsequently murdered in June 1947, presumably by other mobsters who were angry at the lack of return on their investment, although the murderers and their motives were never identified. The investment did pay off soon thereafter, and the casino was highly popular and highly profitable.[9]

Author John Findlay described the Flamingo casino:

Combining Californian with Floridian motifs, the Flamingo presented a new image that announced the desert city's arrival as a leading American resort. Virtually all the hotels that succeeded Siegel's creation incorporated the dual themes of exotic location and luxurious surroundings, even though the specific styles varied. No longer would any major inn be confused with auto courts, as the Last Frontier and El Rancho Vegas had been. No longer could Las Vegas be regarded as a tourist stop. The resort city had advanced in one bound, so to speak, from the backwater of the old West to the cutting edge of a cultural frontier.

After the success of the Flamingo, criminal syndicates from all parts of the country moved in with their money and their gambling skills to play a large role in the shaping of Las Vegas. However, the U.S. Congress became distressed by the rampant and overt graft and corruption of Las Vegas, and Congressman Estes Kefauver initiated congressional hearings on this matter in 1950. As a result of Kefauver's investigations, the state of Nevada cracked down hard on gambling and created strict rules and regulations for the industry to follow.[10]

Atlantic City and Casino Gambling

In the 1970s, Atlantic City, New Jersey, was an old-time seaside resort that had gone to seed. In 1976, New Jersey voters approved a referendum to allow gambling in Atlantic City. The taxes that were to be gained from gambling were to go to senior citizens and disabled individuals. The money actually went into the general fund of the state, which pays for any items the state wishes to pay for, rather than being earmarked for specific groups.

Said Steve Durham and Kathryn Hashimoto, "There literally was dancing in the streets of Atlantic City on election night. The

Figure 2.2 The Las Vegas Strip. *(©AP Images)*

headline in the *Press of Atlantic City* the next morning summed it up: 'CITY REBORN.'"[11] Today Atlantic City is one of the largest casino markets in the United States, and there are about a dozen hotels that offer casino gambling. Celebrities such as Donald Trump have invested in casino hotels, and his property has been sold and resold several times.

According to Durham and Hashimoto, "By the end of 2006, casinos had invested over $12 billion into a tiny city, transforming it from a decaying resort into an exciting, vibrant destination. They had converted the 2,500 acres of developable land into the most valuable real estate in the state of New Jersey. The casino industry also invested more than $1 billion through the Casino Reinvestment Development Authority into projects in Atlantic City that made it a more attractive place to live, to visit and to work. Casino gaming has clearly met the public policy goal of rebuilding Atlantic City."[12]

GAMBLING IN THE TWENTY-FIRST CENTURY

Today many states allow gambling, in the form of state lotteries as well as taxes on casino gambling and gaming establishments run by Native Americans. Internet gambling is another option, although it is an evolving field governed by state and federal laws.

State Lotteries

Lotteries have fallen in and out of favor since early American history, but were largely illegal in the twentieth century until a state lottery was launched in New Hampshire in 1964, after it was enacted into legislation and signed by Governor John King.[13] At first the state lottery was largely decried by other states, but within about a decade, many state government officials realized there was considerable money to be made for their own state coffers with lotteries, and many states established lotteries.

Native American Gaming Establishments

Although most Native American gaming (another word for gambling) sites have not been profitable, some have been hugely successful, such as Foxwoods in Ledyard, Connecticut, a casino owned by the Mashantucket Pequot Indians, which offers 340,000 square feet of casino gambling. With the approval of the United States government, and with certain limitations, federal law allows Native Americans to set up gambling sites that may pay bigger prizes than other local sites. About half of the 562 federally recognized Native American tribes in the United States operate casinos. In general, tribal-run casinos located near urban areas are more likely to succeed than more remotely placed tribal-run casinos.[14]

Figure 2.3 Federal law allows Native Americans to set up gambling sites that may pay bigger prizes than other local sites. About half of the 562 federally recognized Native American tribes in the United States operate casinos. *(©Photo Researchers, Inc.)*

As with states that ran lotteries in the twentieth and twenty-first centuries to increase their revenues, Native Americans largely created their gaming establishments to bring income into their impoverished communities. Gambling by Native Americans is allowed under the Indian Gaming Regulatory Act (IGRA), which was passed in 1988. Prior to the passage of the IGRA, most gambling on Indian reservations was limited to bingo, but after its passage, some Native Americans moved into casino gambling. The IGRA required Native Americans and the states they lived in to negotiate gambling agreements in good faith, which could be appealed to the federal government if the Native Americans believed states failed to negotiate in good faith.

The IGRA divided Native American gambling into three classes. Class I covered social gambling unregulated by either the tribe or the state, such as betting between friends. Class II covered bingo games and simple types of gaming. Class III games included gaming at tables and electronic gambling, which are essentially the types of gambling seen in casinos.

Internet Gambling

The first Internet casino (i-casino) opened in 1995 (Casino.org), and by 1997, there were about 200 sites for i-casinos. Sports betting also took off online at about the same time, and by 2006, there were an estimated 2,500 sites where a person could place wagers on sports, lotteries, bingo games, and i-casinos. Most were (and are) located offshore.[15] Congress became concerned about online gambling, and in 2006 the federal government passed the Unlawful Internet Gambling Enforcement Act (UIGE).

The UIGE prohibited illegal gambling over the Internet in any form and required the Federal Reserve to work with the U.S. Attorney General to create the means to locate illegal bets online. However, the bill has been criticized by some as ineffective, and as of this writing, Congress is seeking to create a new bill overseeing gambling over the Internet.

Some states go beyond the federal law, and specifically ban gambling over the Internet; for example, in Louisiana, it is illegal to place a bet on the Internet with another person who is located within the state, and individuals have been prosecuted, according to Jennifer Chiang in her article on the law and Internet gambling.[16]

Writing about the legal risks of online gambling, Chiang said, "Anyone involved in running, promoting, or using i-gaming sites must consider carefully the risk in traveling to the United States. While those involved in such activities may be in compliance with one state's laws, they may be simultaneously violating another state's laws, potentially subjecting them to arrest warrants and extradition."[17]

RESEARCH INFORMATION IS AVAILABLE TO CASINOS

Unlike in the past, today casino operators who want information on the best ways to attract and keep individuals gambling in their establishments can hire researchers or look at the existing research. For example, researchers have found that people are consistently attracted to and wish to gamble longer in a facility that uses the "playground" casino design versus the gaming design. According to Finlay and colleagues, the playground design is an uncluttered area with high ceilings and the feeling of spaciousness. Flowing water and plants are also present in casinos that use the playground design. Soothing music enhances the playground design, making gamblers want to stay longer, although this type of music is not considered effective in the gaming design. In contrast, the gaming design has low ceilings and few decorations and no fountains, and also is characterized by a mazelike layout.[18]

In a study by Finlay et al. of 484 undergraduates, including 241 males and 243 females, the students, who did not actually gamble, were exposed to professionally made videotapes of casinos with different motifs and questioned about their responses to them. They also evaluated the students based on their level of gambling issues, such that nonproblem gamblers were given a zero rating, low-risk gamblers were rated at 1 or 2, moderate-risk gamblers were rated at 3 to 7, and problem gamblers scored 8 or higher. The researchers looked at how casino design affected gambling levels among these different types of gamblers.

Finlay and colleagues noted that flashing lights decreased the likelihood of responsible gambling (and, conversely, increased the probability of irresponsible gambling) because of the high information load that they present. In addition, the research indicated that females (but not males) are attracted to uncluttered areas, and consequently, they are more likely to gamble beyond their planned level of gambling in such an area. The researchers said, "These results suggest that females should be counseled to avoid gambling in relative isolation. Note that in the case of crowding, a high information load is protective for females."[19]

Of course, individuals who wish to increase the level of gambling can use this information to manipulate the environment in such a way that individuals are more likely to gamble, whether they gamble responsibly or not.

3 Who Are Pathological Gamblers?

Tim, age 22, plans his entire life around gambling. He has a *job, but he's received some bad performance appraisals in the past few years for leaving early and for making personal calls at work to make or check on bets. Tim isn't worried. He only cares about gambling anyway, and the job finances his heavy betting. On Monday night he plays the slots; Tuesdays are for the dog races. Wednesdays are when he buys his lottery tickets at the convenience store. Nothing much goes on Thursdays, which makes him pretty anxious on that day, but then there is Friday, with betting on weekend sports events among his friends, and then more bets on Saturday and Sunday.*

If his losses leave him with very little money, as happens a lot, Tim feels like he has to "chase" those losses by betting even more. Tim is a typical pathological gambler, a young male whose life is centered on the euphoria and excitement that gambling brings to it. Pathological gamblers come in both genders, and all ethnicities, ages, and personalities, but researchers have made some generalizations about this group. For example, males are about twice as likely to become addicted to gambling than females—although some girls and women do gamble excessively.[1] Many gamblers are adults, but often gambling starts in adolescence or young adulthood. In fact, studies have shown that earlier ages of gambling are predictive for lifelong pathological gambling.[2]

Some researchers have found common personality traits among pathological gamblers, such as a high level of **impulsivity** and/or novelty-seeking. Renee Cunningham-Williams and colleagues have found that those gamblers who scored high in novelty-seeking were four times more likely to be pathological gamblers than those individuals who were found to be low in the trait.[3]

CHARACTERISTICS OF PATHOLOGICAL AND PROBLEM GAMBLERS

Some people gamble on the Internet, but the demographics of Internet gamblers are largely the same as those who gamble "off-line": young, male, and African American, with low levels of education and income.[4]

Many studies have shown that pathological gamblers are largely African American, while some are Native American, Asian, or Hispanic.[5] In general, whites have the lowest percentage of pathological gamblers.

Gambling Hotline Study

In a study of Asian-American and white callers to a gambling helpline, Declan T. Barry and colleagues found that the Asian-American callers reported a higher risk of attempted suicides than the white callers, while the white callers reported more issues with alcohol abuse. About 11% of the Asian gamblers reported having attempted suicide, a much higher rate than the 1.5% of the white gamblers who had attempted suicide. However, only 2.9% of the Asian Americans reported problems with alcohol, compared to 14.3% of the white callers.[6] Callers in both groups said they had both family and financial problems caused by their gambling, and they also had a family history of problem gambling.

Lower- and Higher-Income Pathological Gamblers

Although many pathological gamblers are lower-income and unemployed, some do have money and jobs. Some researchers have found major differences between lower-income and higher-income pathological gamblers. For example, in their 2007 article on gambling, Rachel A. Volberg and Matt Wray compared pathological gamblers earning less than $35,000 a year to those earning $35,000 a year or more. They found several distinctive differences: For example, about two-thirds of the lower-income pathological gamblers were male (64%) but among the higher-income gamblers, a much higher percentage—86%—were male. Clearly, although males still represent the majority of pathological gamblers in both social strata, there are more female pathological gamblers among lower-income subjects.[7]

The researchers also found racial disparities related to income. For example, less than half of the lower-income subjects were white (44%), but among the higher-income pathological gamblers, the rate of whites was 77%. In considering pathological gamblers who borrowed from others to finance their gambling, lower-income gamblers were almost twice as likely to borrow from relatives, while the higher-income gamblers were more than twice as likely to borrow the money they needed for gambling from banks or loan companies. In addition, the higher-income gamblers were much more likely to cash in their stocks and bonds (25%) compared to the lower-income gamblers (6%). Obviously the higher-income gamblers had more assets from which to draw in order to support their gambling problem. Of course, if their gambling continues, many of them will wipe out their assets and eventually fall into the lower-income category. See Table 3.1 for more comparisons of pathological gamblers by high and low income.

Figure 3.1 Many studies have found that individuals with only a high school education or less than a high school education have a greater risk for pathological gambling and problem gambling than individuals with a higher education. (*©AP Images*)

Gamblers Generally Are Poorly Educated

Many studies have found that individuals with only a high school education or less than a high school education have a greater risk for pathological gambling and problem gambling than individuals with a higher education. This does not mean that college graduates are never pathological gamblers, but that they have a lower risk for this disorder.[8]

Considering Minority Military Veterans

African Americans are not the only minorities with gambling issues. In a study of 1,228 American Indian military veterans and Hispanic-American veterans and their lifetime prevalence of pathological gambling, Joseph Westermeyer, M.D., Ph.D., and colleagues found a higher than average rate of pathological gambling among both groups.

The American Indian veterans had a 10% lifetime prevalence of pathological gambling and the Hispanic-American veterans' rate was 4.3%, higher than the highest estimates for the national average for pathological gambling, or about 2.5%.[9] It should also be noted that even if military veterans as a group may be more likely to be pathological gamblers (which is unknown), the rate for the American Indians is still extremely high.

In considering the American Indian and Hispanic military veterans as a group, the greatest numbers of pathological gamblers were clustered in the 40 to 49 age group, followed by those who were 50 to 59 years; pathological gamblers represented 11% of those ages 40 to 49 years and 9% of those ages 50 to 59 years. (No veterans either younger than 24 or older than 75 met the criteria for pathological gambling.) This is in sharp contrast to pathological gamblers as a whole, for whom pathological gambling is generally considered a problem of young adults. It is unknown why this older age discrepancy appeared among the veterans.

In comparing military veteran subjects without a pathological gambling problem, the researchers found that they resembled the subjects in the groups with pathological gambling in many

Table 3.1: Characteristics of Pathological Gamblers in the General Population (in percentages)

	LOWER INCOME (N=36)	HIGHER INCOME (N=35)
Demographics		
Male	64	86
White	44	77
High school graduate	54	97
Younger than 30	36	43
Married	33	46
Unemployed	9	3
Borrowing		
Borrowed from relatives	61	31
Borrowed from household	47	29
Borrowed from banks or loan companies	21	46
Cashed bad checks	18	13
Cashed stocks or bonds	6	25

N=Number of individuals surveyed.

Source: AMERICAN BEHAVIORAL SCIENTIST by Rachel Volberg and Matt Wray Copyright © 2007 by SAGE PUBLICATIONS INC JOURNALS. Reproduced with permission of SAGE PUBLICATIONS INC. JOURNALS in the format Tradebook via Copyright Clearance Center.

Rachel A. Volberg and Matt Wray, "Legal Gambling and Problem Gambling as Mechanisms of Social Domination? Some Considerations for Future Research," *American Behavioral Scientist* 51 (2007): p. 70.

ways, but there were some differences; for example, 12.3% of the non-pathological gamblers (139 of 1,135 non-pathological gamblers) were disabled, while 17.2% of the pathological gamblers (16 or 93 subjects) were disabled.[10] Perhaps the presence of a disability increases the risk for gambling, although this topic was not explored any further by the researchers.

The combat status of the veterans appeared particularly significant; of all the pathological gamblers, 68% were combat veterans. In contrast, of all the non-pathological gamblers, only about 8% were combat veterans. This finding may also explain why there was a high rate of post-traumatic stress disorder (PTSD) among the pathological gamblers, since PTSD was more common among combat veterans; for example, PTSD was a problem for about a third (30%) of the pathological gamblers, while it was a problem for only 12% of the non-pathological gamblers.

Internet Gamblers

Some researchers have found that there is a high risk for problem and pathological gambling among those who gamble on the Internet. Robert T. Wood and Robert J. Williams analyzed data from Internet gamblers in the United States, Canada, and other countries. (About 87% were from the U.S. and 10% were from Canada.) Most subjects gambled on computers from their own home, although some gambled while at work.[11]

Using the Canadian Problem Gambling Index (CPGI), the researchers evaluated those who scored 0 as non-problem gamblers, those scoring 1 to 2 as at-risk gamblers, those who scored 3 to 7 as moderate problem gamblers, and those who scored 8 or 9 of 9 scored items as severe problem gamblers (also known as pathological gamblers).

The researchers found a very high rate of problem gambling: about 20% of the subjects were severe problem gamblers and

Figure 3.2 In 2006 the federal government passed the Unlawful Internet Gambling Enforcement Act banning Internet gambling, but the law has been difficult to enforce, as many gambling sites are based offshore. *(©AP Images)*

about 23% were moderate problem gamblers, for a total of 43% with moderate to severe gambling problems. The researchers also noted that the rate of problem gambling among those who used the Internet to gamble was about 10 times greater than the rate of gambling problems found in the general population.

The average time that was spent gambling online was five hours a week, but about 4% gambled online more than 20 hours per week. The researchers also noted that males and individuals of African American and Asian ethnicities were particularly likely to be problem gamblers. In addition, the researchers noted that compared to non-Internet gamblers, those who used the Internet to gamble were not only more at risk for having a gambling problem but they were also at a greater risk for *developing* a problem. This problem may develop because it is easy to use the Internet; it is also anonymous and it may be more affordable than other opportunities to gamble away from home. In addition, online gamblers may lose track of time while gambling on their computers. Many casinos also tend to lack any time cues operating a 24-7 operation and lacking cues to the outside world.

In a study by Nancy M. Petry on Internet gambling, Petry administered the **South Oaks Gambling Screen** to 1,414 adults in medical and dental clinic waiting rooms in Hartford, Connecticut. Only about 7% said that they had ever gambled online, but about 3% said that they frequently wagered on the Internet. Of the subjects who were regular Internet gamblers, two-thirds (66%) were categorized as probable pathological gamblers. The researchers also found that males were more likely to engage in problem gambling on the Internet than females. About 1% of the subjects gambled every day on the Internet.

Petry also found that gambling on the Internet correlated with poor physical and mental health among the gambling subjects, even when controlling for other factors such as age, gender and pathological gambling status. She concluded that either the nature of the Internet itself led to problem gambling behaviors or that those prone to pathological and problem gambling were especially drawn to gambling over the Internet.[12] (Perhaps both possibilities are true.)

Many online gamblers engage in sports betting and playing poker, although pathological gamblers typically prefer games of chance rather than games of skill such as poker. They allow sites to debit their credit cards directly or even their personal bank accounts.

According to the *Los Angeles Times* in late 2010, Congress was considering a bill which would license online gambling sites. The plan was that such sites would include ways to deter minors from gambling by providing age-verification methods (which means were not reported) as well as ban individuals with gambling problems. As of this writing, it is unknown whether the bill will pass but past Congressional efforts to block gambling have failed to date.[13]

RISK FACTORS TOWARD (AND ONE PROTECTIVE FACTOR AGAINST) PATHOLOGICAL GAMBLING

Some researchers have identified risk factors that increased the likelihood of pathological gambling and have also identified one protective factor that *decreased* the risk for pathological gambling. In their study of 1,242 individuals in the St. Louis, Missouri, area, researchers Renee M. Cunningham-Williams and colleagues found that there was a 2.5% lifetime prevalence of pathological gambling among their subjects, and a 12.4% prevalence of sub-threshold gambling (sub-threshold gambling is equal to what others label *problem gambling*).[14] Pathological gamblers were those who met 5 to 10 of the American Psychiatric Association's DSM criteria for pathological gambling, while sub-threshold gamblers met one to four of the same criteria.

The researchers found that having a **novelty-seeking temperament**, or a need for exposure to the new and exciting, was predictive for pathological gambling: Individuals with this personality trait had 4.3 times the risk for becoming pathological gamblers compared to those without it. The researchers also found that among individuals 21 to 34 years old, gamblers who were jobless were 3.6 times more likely to be pathological gamblers than were the subjects who were employed.

The researchers found that "**chasing losses**," or continuing to gamble even when they were losing, was a feature that was commonly present among almost all pathological gamblers (96%). They also found that most pathological gamblers gambled to escape an unhappy mood (90%).[15]

In addition, Cunningham-Williams and colleagues found that when the pathological gamblers were unable to gamble, 28% of the subjects were restless and irritable, compared to less than 1% of the sub-threshold gamblers. Not surprisingly, the frequency of gambling is another factor directly related to pathological gambling, and the researchers found that 61% of the pathological gambler subjects gambled at least three days per week, compared to 12% of the sub-threshold gamblers and to only 1.2% of the recreational (non-problem) gamblers.

Cunningham-Williams and colleagues also found one protective factor that mitigated against gambling issues: Their research showed that attending religious services at least once or twice a month decreased the risk for any type of gambling, including pathological gambling.[16]

FEMALE PATHOLOGICAL GAMBLERS

In general, men are more likely to be pathological gamblers than women, with the exception of incarcerated prisoners, where women are about as equal to gamble as men.[17] Female

Accessibility an Issue with Gamblers

According to a study done for the National Gambling Impact Study Commission in 1999, the presence of a casino less than 50 miles from home (as compared to a casino that is 50 to 250 miles away) is directly associated with twice the prevalence of pathological and problem gambling, based on a telephone survey of adults ages 18 and older as well as a survey of 530 adult patrons of 21 gambling sites. Apparently, closer access raises the risk for gambling problems among those prone to pathological gambling, while casinos farther away are too difficult to access.[18]

Figure 3.3 Female pathological gamblers are more likely than men to play bingo. (*©AP Images*)

pathological gamblers who seek treatment are much less likely than men to be sensation-seeking, while they are more likely than men to play bingo, electronic bingo, or video lotteries.[19]

In her 2009 book on women and problem gambling, *Taking Back Your Life: Women and Problem Gambling*, Diane Rae Davis estimated that more than 5 million females in the United States are problem gamblers. (Davis does not use the term "pathological gambling" but it seems apparent that she is referring to pathological gamblers.) According to Davis, women may gamble to rebel against their female obligations (caretaking responsibilities for house, children, and so forth) and they may also gamble as a means of revenge toward a partner with whom they are angry because of suffering from abuse, neglect, or other reasons.[20]

In an overview of the limited research on female pathological gamblers, Silvia Saboia Martins and colleagues as well as other researchers have found that although a gambling problem develops later in women than in men, pathological gambling may progress more rapidly in women. (This is sometimes referred to as "the telescoping effect.")[21] For example, according to one study by Hermano Tavares and colleagues, the time frame to pass from recreational gambling to problem gambling was only about one year for women, compared to the much longer time frame of 4.6 years for men.[22]

Some Female Gamblers Turn to Crime

If they don't have the money to gamble, some pathological gamblers will turn to crime, including female pathological gamblers. A study by Mary Lou Strachan and Robert Custer in 1989 found that 10% of the 52 female subjects that they interviewed in Las Vegas, Nevada, prostituted themselves so they could obtain enough money to gamble. In this study, most of the subjects were married with children. The researchers also found that other serious problems were linked to gambling, such as suicide attempts (reported by 23% of the subjects), an addiction to illegal drugs (23%), and alcoholism (10%).[23]

Comparing Male and Female Pathological Gamblers

In an Australian study of 4,764 individuals that was published in 2009, the researchers identified 104 pathological gamblers, including 70 men and 34 women. They found distinct differences between the female and male pathological gamblers. For example, the female pathological gamblers were more than twice as likely to seek help for their problem (32%) than the males (13%). Women were also significantly more likely to realize that they had a problem (91.2%) than the men were (74.3%).[24] The researchers did not speculate on why female pathological gamblers were more likely to know they had a problem than men who were pathological gamblers, nor did they speculate on why females were also more likely to seek treatment than male pathological gamblers.

Predicting Which Women May Become Pathological Gamblers

Some researchers have looked at women who already gamble to see if they are at risk for developing pathological gambling, based on their behavior. In a study by Lynn Blinn-Pike and Sheri Lokken Worthy, the researchers studied 179 female undergraduates to compare those who had gambled at casinos to two other groups: those who had gambled elsewhere and those who had never gambled. In this study, 120 women had gambled in a casino, 37 women had never gambled in a casino (but they had gambled), and 22 women had never gambled at all.[25]

None of the non-casino gamblers or the non-gamblers were pathological gamblers, nor were any of these subjects at risk for pathological gambling, based on their scores on the South Oaks Gambling Screen. However, the casino gamblers *were* at risk for pathological gambling based on their scores. The researchers also found that women who gambled at casinos had significantly higher sensation-seeking traits than others. In addition, they had a higher level of alcohol consumption; for example, the casino gamblers reportedly consumed alcohol more frequently in the previous 30 days and had engaged in binge drinking more often than the subjects in the other two groups.

ADOLESCENT PATHOLOGICAL GAMBLERS

Many pathological gamblers start their gambling "careers" in adolescence, betting on cards or dice or Internet games, although most states ban gambling by individuals younger than age 21. In general, gambling is banned by state law for individuals who are either under age 18 or age 21, depending on the state and the type of gambling.[26] To screen adolescents with gambling problems, some researchers use a variation of the South Oaks Gambling Screen (SOGS), which is called the **SOGS-Revised Adolescent (SOGS-RA)**. If an adolescent scores four or higher on this scale this indicates problem gambling, and a score of two or three indicates "at risk" gambling.

In a longitudinal study of 452 urban African-American adolescents that extended from when they entered the first grade and over the next 10 years, the researchers found that for males, gambling behavior was significantly correlated with their teacher ratings of externalizing (acting out) behaviors. For both males and females, gambling was associated with high parent ratings of their children for both hyperactivity and impulsivity.[27]

The Type of Gambling Venue Is Significant

In its 1999 study, the National Opinion Research Center (NORC) at the University of Chicago created its own gambling scale called the NORC DSM Screen for Gambling Programs, or the NODS. Using this scale, they compared the percentage of pathological gamblers who were patrons at the following sites: five casinos in Nevada and Atlantic City, three riverboat gambling sites, two tribal casinos, six lottery outlets, two video lottery terminal locations, and three pari-mutuel betting sites (sites that allow betting on horse races or dog races). The researchers found a high rate of pathological gambling among those using pari-mutuel betting, 25%, followed by a 10.9% rate of pathological gambling on riverboats. The lowest rates were seen with video lottery terminal locations (3.5%) or tribal casinos (4.5%). See Table 3.2 for further information. It is unknown why pathological gamblers seem particularly drawn to some gambling venues over others.

In another study of 1,128 youths ages 14 to 18 who had presented to an inner city hospital emergency room for any reason (58% of whom were African American), the researchers

Table 3.2 Percentage of Gambling Types Based on NODS Lifetime Score, by Gambling Venue

TYPE OF GAMBLER	NV/AC CASINO (5)		RIVERBOATS (3)		TRIBAL CASINO (2)	
	%	N	%	N	%	N
TOTAL	100.0%	149	100.0%	64	100.0%	67
Non-gambler	0.7	1	0	0	0	0
Low-Risk	68.4	102	67.2	43	73.1	49
At-Risk	22.1	33	15.6	10	16.4	11
Problem	3.4	5	6.3	4	6.0	4
Pathological	5.4	8	10.9	4	4.5	3
TYPE OF GAMBLER	LOTTERY OUTLETS (6)		VLT LOCATIONS (2)		PARI-MUTUEL (3)	
TOTAL	100.0%	164	100.0%	30	100.0%	56
Nongambler	0	0	0	0	3.4	2
Low-Risk	78.1	128	70.0	21	33.9	19
At-Risk	12.8	21	23.3	7	23.2	13
Problem	3.7	6	3.3	1	14.3	8
Pathological	5.5	9	3.3	1	25.0	14

Source: Dean Gerstein, et al., "Gambling Impact and Behavior Study: Report to the National Gambling Impact Study Commission," April 1, 1999. Chicago: National Opinion Research Center at the University of Chicago, 1998, p. 36. Available online at http://www2.norc.org/new/pdf/gamble.pdf. Accessed February 26, 2010. Used with permission.

found that the boys were more likely to gamble than the girls. The researchers also found the following factors related to an increased risk for gambling:

- male gender
- African American race
- not attending school
- working for pay
- using alcohol and marijuana
- carrying a weapon
- exhibiting violence

Adolescent gambling is far more common than most people realize. According to Maggie E. Magoon and colleagues, as many as half of all adolescents gamble once a week or more and 4% gamble every day. This is a much higher incidence than among adults. Adolescent gambling is often linked with juvenile delinquency. Gambling problems are higher for incarcerated adolescents, and 18–38% of adolescents may be pathological gamblers, about 9 times the rate for all adolescents and more than 20 times the rate of pathological gambling among adults.[28]

ELDERLY PATHOLOGICAL AND PROBLEM GAMBLERS

Although pathological and problem gambling is more common among younger individuals, some older people may also have a problem with gambling. In a study by Alesia N. Burge and colleagues, the researchers studied 55 problem gamblers over age 65. They were assessed with the South Oaks Gambling Screen and scored an average of 4.3. (Scores of 5 or more indicate pathological gambling.) The researchers found that the median age of starting gambling was 21 years, thus gambling was not a new experience for most of the elderly subjects.[29] (*Median*

Figure 3.4 Older individuals may also be pathological gamblers.

means that half the subjects were younger than age 21 when they started gambling and half were older than age 21.)

For some elderly people, gambling represents a significant part of their recreation, but such individuals are at risk for problem gambling. According to a study of 449 Nevada residents ages 55 years and older, those who said gambling was a major part of their recreation were four times more likely to be at risk for problem gambling than those for whom gambling did not loom large in their lives. The researchers also found that those who earned less than $25,000 a year were significantly more likely to be at risk for problem gambling than those earning more than $50,000 per year. The researchers also found that nonwhites were at greater risk for gambling issues than whites.[30]

Medical and Psychiatric Problems Among Elderly Gamblers

Burge and colleagues compared the elderly subjects who had started gambling early (before age 21) to those who had a late onset of gambling (at age 21 or older), and found that those who started gambling early engaged in more frequent gambling events and had more serious medical and psychiatric problems than the subjects with a later onset of gambling. For example, the problem gamblers with an early onset of gambling had about twice the number of days with medical problems in the past month, or 12.1 days for the early onset gamblers versus 6 days for the late onset gamblers.

Among the early gamblers, 21% had experienced serious **depression** in the past month, compared to 4% of the late gamblers. Twenty-nine percent of the early onset gamblers said they had experienced serious thoughts of suicide, compared to 4% of the late onset gamblers. In addition, 36% of the early onset problem gamblers were currently receiving psychiatric treatment, compared to only 4% of the late onset problem gamblers.

Said the researchers, "These data suggest that gambling that begins in adolescence may be associated with an elevated severity of problems throughout the life span among older adult problem gamblers."[31]

Severity of Gambling May Equate with a Desire for Treatment Among Elderly Gamblers

In a study of 21 pathological gamblers and 10 problem gamblers, all older than 60 years, researchers Robert H. Pietrzak and Nancy M. Petry found that about 75% of the pathological gamblers and 30% of the problem gamblers expressed an interest in treatment for their gambling. The pathological gamblers were lonelier and had more family problems and psychiatric symptoms than the problem gamblers. The researchers noted that a greater percentage of the problem gamblers were retired than of the pathological gamblers. They speculated that the pathological gamblers may have continued to work to pay off their gambling debts.[32]

Comparing an Onset of Late-Life Gambling with Earlier Gambling
In a study of 322 mostly white pathological gamblers by Jon E. Grant and colleagues, the researchers compared gamblers whose pathological gambling had its onset late in life (on or after the age of 55 years) to those whose pathological gambling began at or before age 25 and those whose problematic gambling started when they were 26 to 54 years of age. About 13% (rounded off) of the subjects had late-life pathological gambling, while the majority (67%) had an onset of pathological gambling when they were 26 to 54 years old, and about 20% had an onset of pathological gambling at or before they were 25 years old.[33]

The researchers found that the late-onset gamblers (55 and older) were the most likely subjects to have an anxiety disorder and the least likely to have had a parent with a gambling disorder. Those with a late onset of pathological gambling were the least likely to engage in games of skill, which the authors referred to as "strategic gambling," and were more likely to engage in games of pure chance, such as playing bingo or buying lottery tickets.[34] (The majority of the pathological gambler subjects, as with most pathological gamblers, preferred games of pure chance.)

The late-onset pathological gamblers were also the least likely among such gamblers to have declared **bankruptcy** or written bad checks; for example, about 24% of those whose pathological gambling began at or before age 25 had written bad checks, compared to 16% of those who began at ages 26 to 54 and only 7% of those whose pathological gambling began at ages 55 or older. Among the group whose pathological gambling
(*continues on page 44*)

Table 3.3 Clinical Characteristics of Pathological Gamblers (n=322) Based on Age of Pathological Gambling Onset

	AGE OF PATHOLOGICAL GAMBLING ONSET		
	25 and younger N=63	26 to 54 N=217	55 and older N=42
Duration of pathological gambling from onset to time of study, years, mean (±SD)	17.6 (11.6)	8.4 (5.7)	3.9 (3.7)
Type of gambling, n (%)			
Strategic	42 (66.7)	102 (47.0)	9 (21.4)
Non-strategic	40 (63.5)	178 (82.0)	41 (97.6)
Percent of income lost to gambling (past year), mean (±SD)	43.3 (75.1)	43.2 (57.7)	39.3 (35.0)
Legal problems due to gambling, n (%)			
Any legal	27 (42.9)	66 (30.4)	5 (11.9)
Bankruptcy	18 (28.6)	49 (22.6)	3 (7.1)
Bad checks	15 (23.8)	35 (16.1)	1 (2.4)
Prostitution	(0)	1 (0.5)	0 (0)
Embezzlement	1 (1.6)	5 (2.3)	1 (2.4)
Theft	3 (4.8)	7 (3.2)	0 (0)
Tax issues	1 (1.6)	7 (3.2)	0 (0)
Other problems, n (%)			
Credit card debt	34 (54.0)	130 (59.9)	14 (33.3)
Loss of savings	12 (19.0)	57 (26.3)	6 (14.3)
Loss of inheritance	1 (1.6)	2 (0.9)	0 (0)
Loss of house	5 (7.9)	20 (9.2)	1 (2.4)
Loss of car	3 (4.8)	8 (3.7)	0 (0)
Loss of retirement	2 (3.2)	14 (6.5)	5 (11.9)
Borrowing from family/friends	27 (42.9)	79 (36.4)	6 (14.3)

AGE OF PATHOLOGICAL GAMBLING ONSET			
	25 and younger N=63	26 to 54 N=217	55 and older N=42
Work-related problems	6 (9.5)	37 (17.1)	4 (9.5)
Pawning possessions	13 (20.6)	24 (11.1)	0 (0)
Stealing from family/friends	1 (1.6)	11 (5.1)	0 (0)
Marital problems	13 (20.6)	40 (18.4)	2 (4.8)
Loans	11 (17.5)	46 (21.2)	3 (7.1)
Previous gambling self-help treatment, n (%)			
Gamblers Anonymous	30 (47.6)	88 (40.60	7 (16.7)
Any professional treatment	12 (19.1)	47 (21.6)	6 (14.3)
Lifetime diagnostic history, n (%)			
Any mood disorder	24 (38.1)	81 (37.3)	12 (28.6)
Any anxiety disorder	7 (11.1)	32 (14.7)	16 (38.1)
Any substance use disorder	19 (30.2)	53 (24.4)	9 (21.4)
Family history of alcoholic problems, n (%)			
Father	29 (46.8)	90 (41.9)	13 (31.0)
Mother	6 (9.7)	32 (14.9)	3 (7.1)
Family history of gambling problems, n (%)			
Father	18 (29.0)	51 (23.7)	3 (7.1)
Mother	18 (29.0)	42 (19.5)	4 (9.5)

N=Number of individuals.

Figures in parentheses are percentages.

Reprinted from the *Journal of Psychiatric Research* 43, no. 4, Jon E. Grant, J.D., M.D., et al. "Late-Onset Pathological Gambling: Clinical Correlates and Gender Differences" 2009, with permission from Elsevier.

(*continued from page 41*)

started early, 29% had declared bankruptcy, compared to 23% for those whose gambling began at ages 26 to 54 and 7% of those who started gambling late in life. (See Table 3.3 for more information.)

Older individuals were also the least likely to have sought help for their pathological gambling, and only about 17% of the older gamblers had gone to the Gamblers Anonymous support group, compared to 41% of those with an onset of pathological gambling in middle age and 48% of those who had an early onset of pathological gambling. The late-onset pathological gamblers had the lowest rates of seeking any professional treatment—14%—compared to 22% of those with a middle-aged onset of pathological gambling and 19% of those whose pathological gambling started early.

This chapter provided basic information on individuals who are the most at risk for problem or pathological gambling, ranging from adolescents at risk to senior citizens as well as males and females, those with an early or late onset of gambling, and other demographic groups.

Causes of
Pathological Gambling

Carol, 30, is a pathological gambler, just like both her mother and her father. She has been in jail several times for petty thefts when she shoplifted some items from a department store and was caught, and then she did the same thing again at the same chain in a different location. Both of her parents have been in and out of jail since Carol can remember and they are heavy drinkers and smokers, as is Carol.

Many theories exist about why people become pathological gamblers, including theories about the effects of **neurochemicals** (brain chemicals) generated just prior to or during gambling, the impact of both genetics and the environment, addiction models, and other explanations. Sometimes combined effects seem apparent. For example, the pathological gambler may have a parent who was a pathological gambler, thus an individual may be genetically "loaded" for compulsive gambling, as well as having an environmental risk because of exposure to gambling in childhood. He or she may also have inherited a neurochemical makeup that predisposes an individual to gambling.

GENETIC RISKS

Some researchers have identified a specific gene linked to gambling; for example, D.E. Comings and colleagues found that some genetic variations were significantly prevalent in pathological gamblers.[1] In their article summarizing the **genetic risk** of pathological gambling, Daniela S.S. Lobo and James L. Kennedy analyzed 18 research studies on this topic. The studies that they analyzed found that up to 60% of the causes of pathological gambling are likely to be inherited factors, at least in part based on twin studies of adults.

Lobo and Kennedy also reported on genetic links associated with pathological gambling. Other genetic links have been found to impulsive behavior, primarily in women, and pathological gambling in men.[2]

Louise Sharpe says that a genetic vulnerability to pathological gambling may also be linked to specific psychological traits like impulsivity. Impulsivity is often an inherited trait, as it is found among individuals with **attention deficit/hyperactivity disorder** (ADHD).[3]

Both children and adults can have ADHD; an estimated 4.1% of adults ages 18 to 44 years in the United States have ADHD, according to the National Institute of Mental Health (NIMH).[4] Of course, this does not mean that individuals with ADHD inevitably become pathological gamblers. It means instead that the risk for gambling may be elevated in individuals with ADHD compared to those without ADHD, as is discussed in the chapter on other psychiatric problems that frequently occur alongside pathological gambling.

COMBINED INFLUENCES OF GENES AND ENVIRONMENT

In addition to a possible genetic risk for pathological gambling, the environmental influence on a growing child is clearly important as well. Researchers Liana Schreiber and colleagues studied the characteristics of pathological gamblers who had a parent with a gambling problem, reporting their findings in the *American Journal on Addictions* in 2009. It was clear from their research that the environment in which the gamblers were raised had a profound impact on them. The researchers also postulated that heredity played a role as well.

The researchers found that "The association between having a problem gambling parent and a father with an alcohol use disorder also suggests a possible genetic transmission of addictions. Data from the Vietnam Era Twin registry suggests that genetic factors may account for between 35% and 54% of the liability for PG [pathological gambling] symptomatology and that there are common genetic and environmental contributions to PG and alcohol dependence."[5]

The researchers studied 517 pathological gamblers, including 172 subjects with at least one parent who was a problem gambler during the subjects' childhood. The subjects were told that a problem gambler was a person who had caused social, financial, marital, or occupational problems that the subject had noticed, or was a parent who had told the subject that he or she had lost control over gambling. Of the subjects with a gambling parent, about 44% said that it was only their father with the problem, 33% said it was only their mother with the problem, and 23% said both parents had gambling problems.[6]

The researchers found that pathological gamblers with and without parents who were problem gamblers were similar in many ways, but there also were some key differences. For example, the female pathological gamblers who had a parent with a gambling problem were more likely to have a father with an alcohol use disorder (either alcohol abuse or alcohol dependence) than the females without a problem gambling parent. In addition, the females with a gambling parent had a significantly earlier onset of their gambling than did the females without a gambling parent; however, this finding did not hold true for males.

Male pathological gamblers who had a parent with a gambling problem were more likely to have experienced legal problems linked to their gambling than those without such a parent.

Figure 4.1 Recent studies have indicated a link between some problem gamblers and their parents' gambling problems. *(©AP Images)*

They were also more likely to have a father with an alcohol use disorder, compared to the male pathological gamblers whose parents did not have problem gambling.

The researchers also found that pathological gamblers who had a problem-gambling parent had significantly higher rates of using nicotine daily, and the researchers speculated that this could mean that individuals who are genetically prone to addiction may also have a predisposition to gamble and smoke excessively.

Lobo and Kennedy noted that some studies have found a correlation between an exposure to traumatic events and a subsequent development of pathological gambling. For example, research has indicated that an increased number of traumatic events is related to an elevated risk for the development of pathological gambling. Researchers also found that of all traumatic events that may occur in childhood, child neglect had the greatest correlation with pathological gambling in adulthood. In addition, among adults who experienced traumatic events in adulthood, rape had the strongest correlation to pathological gambling.[7]

THE ADDICTION MODEL

Although pathological gambling is categorized as an impulse control disorder by the American Psychiatric Association rather than an addictive disorder, some experts on gambling such as Jon E. Grant, M.D., defend their belief that pathological gamblers are "addicted" to gambling, similarly to how individuals are addicted to alcohol or drugs. They note that with both substance dependence and pathological gambling, there are symptoms of tolerance, or needing more alcohol, drugs, or gambling to achieve the same level of euphoria. Experts who equate pathological gambling with addiction note that pathological gamblers exhibit symptoms of withdrawal when they cannot gamble; for example,

The Type of Gambling and the Possible Motivation

Some researchers such as Louise Sharpe have speculated that individuals who develop gambling problems with electronic gaming machines are also those who have high levels of anxiety and stress in their lives, and they seek to avoid this stress by reinterpreting gaming stress as excitement. In contrast, Sharpe says that people who concentrate on horse racing or casino gambling are often bored with their lives, and they seek the excitement and the stimulation that these activities bring to their nervous system.[8]

becoming anxious and irritable. In addition, addicts frequently have tried to stop their addictive behaviors and have failed, as have pathological gamblers. Last, addiction impedes the addict's normal life activities at work and with their families, as pathological gambling does to gamblers.[9]

It is also true that some drugs that have been used successfully to treat addiction, such as **naltrexone**, have been found effective in treating pathological gamblers. Grant and colleagues note that pathological gambling may be perceived as a behavioral addiction, in that there are repeated instances of compulsive behavior despite negative consequences and the individual has decreasing control over his or her behavior. In addition, the pathological gambler experiences a craving to gamble beforehand and also a euphoric thrill when the gambling actually occurs.[10]

THE CONTINUUM THEORY

Some experts believe that pathological gambling and subclinical pathological gambling (which many experts refer to as *problem gambling* to differentiate it from pathological gambling) are actually the same disorder, but on a continuum, with non-gambling at one end, problem gambling further along the continuum, and then pathological gambling being the worse disorder at the far right of the continuum.[11] This theory may be compared to the contention of some experts that alcohol abuse and alcoholism lie on the same continuum.

BRAIN NEUROCHEMICALS

The rush that gambling brings a pathological gambler may itself be the major draw, which also means that it is likely that they particularly enjoy the release of mood-elevating brain chemicals, such as serotonin and dopamine, as well the surge of adrenaline that occurs with exciting events. For some, gambling generates a surge in release of euphoric chemicals, a "rush" in

positive feelings. It is this natural high that may draw pathological gamblers to gamble again and again. For example, A. Roy
and colleagues noted significantly higher levels of norepineph-
rine in the cerebrospinal fluids of gamblers.[12]

Some individuals have a genetic propensity for the release of
brain chemicals such as serotonin and dopamine during certain
behaviors, such as impulsive actions, including pathological
gambling. The reality is that it is very hard (and may be impos-
sible) to tease out which aspects of a person's psyche are caused
by genetics and which by environment, and further study will
likely underline the importance of both areas of influence.

PARKINSON'S DISEASE AND PATHOLOGICAL GAMBLING

Some researchers have found that some individuals diagnosed
with **Parkinson's disease** have developed pathological gambling.
Parkinson's disease is a degenerative brain disorder that causes
slowed and uncontrolled movements as well as impaired balance and coordination. The new onset of pathological gambling
in some Parkinson's patients is apparently *not* caused by the disease itself but rather by a type of medication that is sometimes
used to treat the disease: dopamine agonists (dopamine block-
ers), such as pramipexole (Mirapex) or ropinirole (Requip).

When the medication dosage was reduced or discontinued
among those with gambling problems, the gambling abated.
The medications also apparently induced a hypersexuality in
some patients, and this behavior also ended when the dosage
was cut back or the drug was discontinued. The behavior was
not seen among Parkinson's patients who were taking either
carbidopa or levodopa, other common medications used to
treat Parkinson's disease.[13]

This chapter covered basic theories about the causes of
pathological gambling, such as the impact of genetics and environment as well as other potential causes.

5 Other Psychiatric and Health Issues

Jake, age 35, gambled nearly every day, and on the days that he did not gamble, he felt actively apprehensive, like things were somehow "off." Jake thought maybe he was hitting the bottle a little bit too frequently, and several times he had woken up in a place with no idea of how he had arrived there. So maybe his alcoholic blackouts were the main problem. He also felt very depressed. As with many pathological gamblers, Jake has a problem with gambling as well as problems with substance abuse and/or psychiatric disorders.

Psychiatric disorders commonly accompany pathological gambling, including abuse or dependence on alcohol, nicotine, and drugs, as well as some psychiatric disorders such as depression, **anxiety disorders**, and attention deficit/hyperactivity disorder (ADHD). There are also health risks that are common with pathological gamblers, who frequently neglect their health since their highest priority is gambling rather than eating right, getting enough sleep, or seeing the doctor if they become sick.

Ronald Kessler and colleagues found that the onset and continuance of problematic gambling was predicted by earlier problems with the presence of mood disorders, anxiety disorders, and substance use disorders. In fact, nearly half (49%) of the subjects had been treated in the past for psychiatric disorders or substance abuse, although none were treated for gambling disorders.[1] The sad reality is that it very seldom occurs to most therapists to ask patients about possible gambling issues, nor do their patients bring up the topic. Thus, it is ignored, even though pathological gambling takes an enormous emotional and financial toll on its sufferers.

SUBSTANCE ABUSE AND DEPENDENCE

Many researchers have found that alcohol and nicotine are the substances that are most often linked to pathological gambling.[2,3] In addition, researchers have found that substance use disorders combined with gambling are more common among males than females.[4] Researchers have also found that those who are already diagnosed with substance use disorders are more likely to be pathological gamblers.[5]

According to an analysis by Nancy Petry and colleagues of data from the National Epidemiological Survey on Alcohol and Related Conditions, an estimated 73% of pathological gamblers meet the criteria for alcohol abuse or alcoholism and 38% meet the criteria for drug abuse or drug addiction.[6] (Some individuals abuse both alcohol and drugs. Alcohol is frequently served for free to gamblers in casinos, which may exacerbate their risk for alcohol abuse and alcoholism.)

In addition, as noted by Edward Gottheil and colleagues, pathological gamblers share many of the same characteristics as those with substance use disorders. The authors wrote, "Common correlates include gender (men), athletes, positive family history, early age of onset, presence of mood disorder (especially depression and anxiety), sensation seeking and impulsivity, social norms, and low academic performance."[7]

Some researchers have found that when individuals have both pathological gambling and substance abuse issues, often the substance abuse came first, particularly in the case of alcohol, nicotine, or marijuana dependence; more than half

Figure 5.1 According to one study, an estimated 73% of pathological gamblers meet the criteria for alcohol abuse or alcoholism. (©istockphoto)

and up to two-thirds of the subjects were dependent on these substances prior to their problem with pathological gambling. However, in some cases, it was the pathological gambling that came first, as in 70% of the cases of individuals with an amphetamine or cocaine dependence.[8] The reasons for these disparities are unknown.

OTHER PSYCHIATRIC DISORDERS

Pathological gamblers commonly have other psychiatric diagnoses. R.A. McCormick and colleagues found that 76% of treatment-seeking gamblers also met the criteria for a major mood disorder, such as depression or bipolar disorder.[9] Other researchers have found that problem gamblers are three times more likely than those without problem gambling to fit the criteria for alcoholism or depression.[10] Some researchers have found that the presence of depression, anxiety, or suicidal tendencies are predictive for pathological gambling.[11] The authors also used the Patient Health Questionnaire (PHQ) and the Temperament and Character Inventory (TCI) to evaluate the subjects with regard to depression, novelty seeking, and so forth. The results of the study are summarized in Table 5.1.

Renee Cunningham-Williams and colleagues found that pathological gamblers are more likely than other individuals to report having thoughts of their own death or to have attempted suicide, and they were also significantly more likely to have ever taken psychiatric medications.[12] See Table 5.1 for more information based on the psychiatric status of subjects who took the GAM-IV-S, an instrument that was devised by the researchers who did the study and also based on the *DSM* criteria for gambling. As can be seen from the table, nearly a third (29%) of the pathological gamblers had thoughts of their own death or self-harm, compared to 10% of the problem gamblers.

Depression

Many pathological gamblers are chronically depressed; in fact, some report that they gamble in order to improve a low or depressed mood. As can be seen from Table 5.1, 19% of the pathological gamblers had major depression compared to 5% or less of the subjects in all the other categories described.

Anxiety Disorders

Anxiety disorders are psychiatric diagnoses such as specific phobia disorder, generalized anxiety disorder, and post-traumatic stress disorder. Cunningham-Williams and colleagues found that in 86% of the cases of subjects who had both pathological gambling and phobia, the phobia appeared before the pathological gambling.[13] Perhaps the pathological gambling developed as a way for the individual to try to ignore the phobia, although further study is needed to determine causes and effects.

Antisocial Personality Disorder (ASPD)

Another disorder that is common among pathological gamblers studied by Cunningham-Williams and colleagues was **antisocial personality disorder** (ASPD), a disorder that is characterized by criminal acts and a disregard for the rights of others. A person with antisocial personality disorder is aware of social behavioral norms but who violates them anyway, believing that they don't

Table 5.1 Psychiatric and Substance Use Correlates by GAM-IV-S© Gambling Status

Full sample	Full Sample n (Weighted %)	Non-gamblers n (%)	Recreational gamblers [a] n (%)	Sub-threshold gamblers[b] n (%)	PGD[c] n (%)
Patient Health Questionaire					
Major depression	39 (4)	19 (5)	11 (3)	6 (4)	3 (19)
Ever taken psychiatric medicine	268 (29)	109 (26)	117 (28)	32 (29)	7 (38)
Generalized anxiety	42 (5)	17 (5)	13 (3)	9 (6)	3 (19)
Binge eating	67 (7)	24 (6)	26 (7)	13 (12)	3 (12)
Thoughts of death/harm	62 (7)	26 (7)	21 (6)	10 (10)	5 (29)
Suicide attempts	54 (6)	27 (7)	15 (4)	9 (9)	3 (13)
Alcohol abuse/dependence	175 (19)	44 (12)	98 (25)	28 (29)	5 (26)
Tobacco dependence	177 (20)	51 (13)	84 (19)	34 (31)	8 (38)

N=Number of individuals.
[a] Recreational gamblers = gamblers without *DSM-IV* pathological gambling criteria.
[b] Sub-threshold = gamblers meeting 1–4 *DSM-IV* pathological gambling criteria.
[c] PGD (Pathological gamblers) = gamblers meeting 5–10 criteria, thus being diagnosed with pathological gambling disorder.
Adapted from Renee M. Cunningham-Williams, et al., "Prevalence and Predictors of Pathological Gambling: Results from the St. Louis Personality, Health and Lifestyle (SLPHL) Study," *Journal of Psychiatric* Research 39, no. 4 (2005). Reprinted with permission from Elsevier.

apply to him or her. About 30% of the pathological gamblers had ASPD, compared to about 7% of the non-pathological gamblers with this disorder.[14]

ADHD
Some research has shown that problem gambling is sometimes linked to a diagnosis with attention deficit/hyperactivity disorder (ADHD). In a longitudinal study of 235 young adults ages 18 to 24, including 179 males and 56 females, the researchers found that the young adults who reported ADHD symptoms in their childhoods that persisted into adulthood had a greater risk for gambling problems than the subjects whose ADHD did not persist into adulthood or the subjects who never had ADHD symptoms at all.[15]

HEALTH RISKS OF PATHOLOGICAL GAMBLERS
In addition to their greater risk for psychiatric problems, pathological gamblers also have an increased risk for a variety of serious health problems. Andrew V. Pasternak IV, M.D., and Michael F. Fleming, M.D., studied 1,051 patients who were anonymously surveyed and screened for gambling disorders at three Wisconsin primary care clinics. The researchers found that more than 80% of the patients had gambled and 6.2% of them met the criteria for gambling disorders, which is about twice the norm that is found in the general public.[16] They also found that those with gambling disorders had lower ratings of their own health and also had a higher rate of reporting severe symptoms of backache and heartburn than the other subjects.[17]

In a study by Benjamin J. Morasco and colleagues based on 575 subjects in an urban environment, the researchers found that 10.6% met the lifetime criteria for pathological gambling, an even higher rate than found by Pasternak and Fleming. They also classified an additional 5% of the subjects as problem gamblers; thus nearly 16% had gambling issues. The researchers found that the pathological and problem gamblers reported significantly worse physical and emotional health than those without gambling problems.[18] In addition, they found that the prevalence of problem and pathological gambling was linked to males, nonwhites, and those who were disabled.

The researchers said, "Although other data support the relationship between gambling severity and health functioning, the causal mechanism remains unknown. Individuals with some medical conditions and physical limitations (e.g., arthritis, obesity, and pain disorders) may be more prone to participating in gambling activities, as it is a recreational pursuit that does not require much physical ability. For individuals with some mental health disorders, gambling may be a mechanism used to cope with psychological symptoms. Shared epidemiological factors may also account for this association, as both gambling disorders and many health conditions are associated with nicotine dependence and alcohol and substance use."[19]

This chapter covered psychiatric issues that often co-exist in individuals who are pathological gamblers, such as alcohol dependence, anxiety, depression and other disorders.

Social and Legal Problems Caused by Gambling

6

Everyone said Tony, 35, was a really nice guy when he wasn't gambling. But when he hit a losing streak, and also when he had lost big and downed some extra shots to ease the pressure, Tony became physically, emotionally, and verbally abusive to others. The state protective services worker had been called to Tony's house a few times because the children had far too many bruises and broken bones for normal kids. Tony had explained that those clumsy kids of his sure fell down a lot. When they were interviewed separately, the children were afraid to say what had really happened to them—that Tony beat them when he was in a rage and he was very angry, very often. The social worker said that the next time she came to the house, the kids were leaving with her to go to foster homes.

Pathological gambling and problem gambling are often linked to criminal behavior, and many prison inmates are also pathological gamblers. In addition, the family of the pathological gambler is also directly affected by this behavior, and some children of gamblers suffer from physical and emotional abuse and neglect, as do their adult partners. The risk for **violence** is elevated among many pathological gamblers, especially those in trouble with law enforcement.

PATHOLOGICAL GAMBLING: EFFECTS ON THE FAMILY

When one or more family members engage in problem or pathological gambling, all family members usually suffer.

They have an increased risk for enduring physical and emotional abuse, financial hardship, and the destruction of personal relationships. They may also suffer from reduced physical and mental health. For example, in a study in Norway of 3,483 subjects, researchers identified about 2% of this population as "concerned significant others" (CSOs) whose family members or relatives were pathological gamblers.[1]

These individuals were compared with the non-CSO subjects. The researchers found that 46.3% of the CSOs reported a worsening of their family situation, compared to only 1% of the non-CSOs. In addition, nearly two-thirds (64.9%) of the

Table 6.1 Reported Effects* of Gambling in the Family among Concerned Significant Others (CSO) and non-CSO

	NON-CSO (%)	CSO (%)
Number	3,412	70
Improvement of family financial situation	1.4	1.4
Worsening of family financial situation	1.0	46.3
Less contact with family and friends	0.2	8.7
Conflicts in the family	1.2	64.9
Reduced mental health (anxiety, depression)	0.3	16.6
Reduced physical health (muscle tension, headache, stomachache, etc.)	0.3	17.8

*Respondents were asked to answer the question: "What has it meant to you that someone in your family is gambling/has been gambling?" (multiple response question)

Source: BMC PUBLIC HEALTH ONLINE by Hanne Gro Wenzel, Anita Oren, and Inger Johanne Bakken. Copyright © 2008 by BIOMED CENTRAL LTD. Reproduced with permission of BIOMED CENTRAL LTD. In the format Tradebook via Copyright Clearance Center.

CSOs reported conflicts in the family, compared to 1.2% of the non-CSOs. The CSOs also had a much higher rate of reduced mental health and reduced physical health than the non-CSOs. See Table 6.1 for more details.

In another study on gambling performed by the National Opinion Research Center at the University of Chicago, the researchers performed phone interviews and found significant differences between pathological gamblers, problem gamblers, and those without a gambling problem in terms of such life-changing events as divorce, getting arrested, declaring bankruptcy, and so forth.[2] For example, as can be seen from Table 6.2, 54% of the pathological gamblers were divorced, compared to 40% of the problem gamblers and only 18% of those without gambling problems. Nineteen percent of the pathological gamblers had declared bankruptcy, compared to 10% of the

Table 6.2 Impact of Pathological Gambling and Problem Gambling On Gamblers and Their Families

IMPACT	PATHOLOGICAL GAMBLERS	PROBLEM GAMBLERS	THOSE WITHOUT GAMBLING PROBLEMS
Divorced	54%	40%	18%
Declared Bankruptcy	19%	10%	4%
Lost a job/fired in the past year	14%	11%	3%
Ever been incarcerated	21%	10%	Less than 1%

Data compiled from information in the following source: Dean Gerstein, et al., "Gambling Impact and Behavior Study: Report to the National Gambling Impact Study Commission," April 1, 1999. Chicago: National Opinion Research Center at the University of Chicago, 1998, pp. 44, 46, 49. Available online at http://www2.norc.org/new/pdf/gamble.pdf. Accessed February 26, 2010.

problem gamblers and only 4% of those without problem gambling issues.

VIOLENT BEHAVIOR

Violence is common among pathological gamblers, who are more likely to abuse their partners, their children, and others than are non-pathological gamblers. Pathological gambling increases the risk of severe **child abuse** by about 13 times and it increases the risk of severe marital violence by about 20 times. In addition, the perpetration of acts of dating violence increases by at least 6 times when the individual (usually a male) is a pathological gambler.[3]

One study that looked at violence in conjunction with psychiatric disorders also found that the odds of violent behavior increased with pathological gambling; the pathological gamblers were 2.54 times more likely to have committed a violent act since age 15 compared to those without this disorder. Among those with pathological gambling and at least one other psychiatric disorder, nearly 29% had committed violent acts since age 15. The researchers estimated that almost a quarter of a million people (244,152) with pathological gambling and another psychiatric disorder had committed violent acts.[4] Since comorbidity (having two or more disorders) is common among pathological gamblers, this percentage is a very sobering statistic that deserves to be highlighted.

FINANCIAL HARDSHIP

Pathological gamblers and their families often suffer from severe financial losses, and research has shown that about 22% have lost their homes or cars because of gambling losses. In addition, one study showed that nearly half (44%) of pathological gamblers have no savings and no retirement income.[5] In a study by Jon E. Grant and colleagues on pathological gamblers who had declared personal bankruptcy, the researchers compared 93 pathological gamblers who were bankrupt and compared them to 424 pathological gamblers who had not declared bankruptcy. Of the gamblers who had declared bankruptcy, the average debt at the time was $33,086.96.[6]

They found some significant differences between the two groups; for example, the bankrupt gamblers were more likely than the non-bankrupt gamblers to be single and to have started gambling earlier in life. They also were more likely to have legal problems; for example, about 38% of the gamblers who had declared bankruptcy had written bad checks, compared to about 14% of those gamblers who did not file for bankruptcy. The bankrupt gamblers were twice as likely to have had work problems that were caused by gambling (23%) as the non-bankrupt gamblers (12%) and nearly twice as likely to have had marital problems (61%) compared to the non-bankrupt gamblers (38%). In addition, they were nearly five times more likely to have lost their house because of gambling (17%) compared to the non-bankrupt gamblers (3.5%).

The researchers also found that the bankrupt subjects had a higher rate of both depression and substance abuse and they were more likely to use nicotine daily. For example, 30% of the bankrupt

Gambling Led to Infant Death

A 26-year-old female army sergeant pleaded guilty to involuntary manslaughter after she was charged with homicide by child abuse in 1997. She left her 10-day-old infant, Joy, alone in a hot car for seven hours while she played video poker in Savannah, Georgia. Experts say that the baby died after two hours in the car. Her husband said that he didn't blame her and that she had an addiction. A year later, the state banned video poker gambling at the urging of the governor.[7]

gamblers had major depressive disorder, compared to 13% of the non-bankrupt gamblers. In addition, 31% of the bankrupt gamblers had a problem with alcohol abuse or dependence, compared to 17% of the non-bankrupt gamblers, nearly double the rate.

SUPPORT FOR FAMILIES HARMED BY GAMBLING

Gam-Anon is a sister organization to Gamblers Anonymous for others who have been harmed by the behavior of a compulsive gambler. Gam-Anon International is based in Whitestone, New York, and can be reached at P.O. Box 157, Whitestone, NY 11357. Its phone number is (718) 352-1671 and its Web site is www.gam-anon.org.

PATHOLOGICAL GAMBLERS AND CRIME

Pathological gambling and problem gambling are common issues among criminals, and an estimated one-third of all criminals are pathological gamblers or problem gamblers, the highest known rate of any population. In addition, about half of all the crimes that were committed by incarcerated pathological gamblers and problem gamblers were done to support their gambling habit.[8] According to the U.S. Department of Justice, about a third of arrested individuals who were identified as pathological gamblers admitted that they had committed a robbery in the past year, and 13% had assaulted someone for money. In addition, pathological gamblers were more likely to sell drugs than others arrested for crimes.[9]

Taking a Look at Imprisoned Adults and Gambling

In the general population, men are more likely than women to be pathological gamblers; however, when they are incarcerated, both men and women are equally likely to gamble to excess.[10]

In a study by the Department of Justice on arrested individuals in Las Vegas, an area with a great deal of gambling, and

Des Moines, Iowa, a Midwestern city, the researchers found that about 1 in 10 arrestees in Las Vegas and 1 in 25 in Des Moines were either pathological or problem gamblers, about three to five times greater than the level of problematic gambling in the general public. In addition, the researchers found that more than a third of the pathological gamblers in both Las Vegas and Des Moines had been arrested at least once for a felony (major crime).

Interestingly, the researchers found that on average, the pathological gamblers said that they became criminals before they developed a gambling problem, committing their first crime at about age 21, then developing an alcohol or drug problem by age 24 and subsequently developing a gambling problem.[11]

In a comprehensive analysis of studies of gambling problems among criminal offenders in the United States, the United Kingdom, Australia, and New Zealand, Robert J. Williams and colleagues found that a third of the inmates were pathological gamblers, which they noted was the highest rate among any population. In addition, they reported that about half the crimes of pathological and problem gamblers were committed to support gambling. Yet very few correctional facilities screen inmates for gambling. If all these inmates were screened and treated, it would not eradicate their crimes, since the other half of the crimes they commit were not related to gambling; however, it would likely decrease the crime rate once they were released from prison because of their treatment for gambling problems while incarcerated.[12]

Incarcerated Adolescents

The prevalence of pathological gambling is as high as 38% among incarcerated adolescents, about 9 times greater than the rate of pathological gamblers among nonincarcerated

(*continues on page 68*)

Questions to Ask Yourself if You Live with a Compulsive Gambler

The following questions are offered by the Gam-Anon organization to help individuals decide if they may be living with a compulsive gambler:

If there is a gambling problem in your home, the Gam-Anon family group may be able to help you cope with it. If you are living with a compulsive gambler, you will answer "yes" to at least six of the following questions.

1. Do you find yourself constantly bothered by bill collectors?
2. Is the person in question often away from home for long, unexplained periods of time?
3. Does this person ever lose time from work due to gambling?
4. Do you feel that this person cannot be trusted with money?
5. Does the person in question faithfully promise that he or she will stop gambling; beg, plead for another chance, yet gamble again and again?
6. Does this person ever gamble longer than he or she intended to, until the last dollar is gone?
7. Does this person immediately return to gambling to try to recover losses, or to win more?
8. Does this person ever gamble to get money to solve financial difficulties or have unrealistic expectations that gambling will bring the family material comfort and wealth?
9. Does this person borrow money to gamble with or to pay gambling debts?

10. Has this person's reputation ever suffered due to gambling, even to the extent of committing illegal acts to finance gambling?

11. Have you come to the point of hiding money needed for living expenses, knowing that you and the rest of the family may go without food and clothing if you do not?

12. Do you search this person's clothing or go through his or her wallet when the opportunity presents itself, or otherwise check on his or her activities?

13. Does the person in question hide his or her money?

14. Have you noticed a personality change in the gambler as his or her gambling progresses?

15. Does the person in question consistently lie to cover up or deny his or her gambling activities?

16. Does this person use guilt induction as a method of shifting responsibilities for his or her gambling upon you?

17. Do you attempt to anticipate this person's moods, or try to control his or her life?

18. Does this person ever suffer from remorse or depression due to gambling, sometimes to the point of self-destruction?

19. Has the gambling ever brought you to the point of threatening to break up the family unit?

20. Do you feel that your life together is a nightmare?

(*continued from page 65*)

adolescents and about 20 times greater than the rate among nonincarcerated adults who are pathological gamblers. Males and females in the juvenile justice system have about the same level of compulsive gambling. In addition, researchers have found that pathological gambling and problem gambling are associated with the commission of delinquent acts such as stealing or vandalism. Adolescents can be screened with the Twenty Questions offered by Gamblers Anonymous for adult members (as provided in Chapter 7) or they may be screened with the South Oaks Gambling Screen–Revised for Adolescents (SOGS–RA).[13]

This chapter covered the consequences of pathological gambler to the family of the gambler, such as violence, child abuse, severe financial losses and other major problems.

Treatment: Support Groups, Medication, and Therapy

It wasn't until several years after his marriage failed, his kids said that they hated him, and there seemed like there was nothing good left in his life that Jim, 41, decided that he really needed to get rid of his severe gambling problem. But how? His doctor had recommended attending Gamblers Anonymous meetings and he also said there were some medications that Jim could try. In addition, the physician also said therapy helped a lot of people with a gambling problem. Jim didn't know if one or any of these things would work, but he had nothing to lose, since everything he cared about (other than gambling) was gone. And lately, even gambling no longer held the old thrill for him.

Pathological gamblers can recover if they sincerely wish to recover, with the help of medication and therapy as well as the assistance of and active participation in self-help groups such as Gamblers Anonymous.

GAMBLERS ANONYMOUS

Gamblers Anonymous is an international support group that is modeled on Alcoholics Anonymous and its Twelve Steps, such as acknowledging one's own inability to resolve the gambling (or alcohol) problem. And as with Alcoholics Anonymous, the organization was launched by two sufferers—in this case, two men whose gambling was out of control. These men began meeting in 1957, and today there are Gamblers Anonymous groups throughout the United States and the world. The organization is based in Los Angeles at P.O. Box 17173, Los Angeles, CA 90017. Their phone number is (213) 386-8789, their Web site is at www.gamblersanonymous.org, and their e-mail address is isomain@gamblersanonymous.org.

Twenty Questions of Gamblers Anonymous

Gamblers Anonymous offers the following questions to anyone who may have a gambling problem. These questions are provided to help the individual decide if he or she is a compulsive gambler and wants to stop gambling.

1. Did you ever lose time from work or school due to gambling?
2. Has gambling ever made your home life unhappy?
3. Did gambling affect your reputation?
4. Have you ever felt remorse after gambling?
5. Did you ever gamble to get money with which to pay debts or otherwise solve financial difficulties?
6. Did gambling cause a decrease in your ambition or efficiency?
7. After losing did you feel you must return as soon as possible and win back your losses?
8. After a win did you have a strong urge to return and win more?
9. Did you often gamble until your last dollar was gone?
10. Did you ever borrow to finance your gambling?

Gamblers Anonymous uses the term "compulsive gambling" to define the problem with which they help others rather than calling it pathological gambling, and individuals decide for themselves whether such a problem exists in their lives. With Gamblers Anonymous, a primary goal is to abstain from all gambling.

11. Have you ever sold anything to finance gambling?

12. Were you reluctant to use "gambling money" for normal expenditures?

13. Did gambling make you careless of the welfare of yourself or your family?

14. Did you ever gamble longer than you had planned?

15. Have you ever gambled to escape worry, trouble, boredom, or loneliness?

16. Have you ever committed, or considered committing, an illegal act to finance gambling?

17. Did gambling cause you to have difficulty in sleeping?

18. Do arguments, disappointments, or frustrations create within you an urge to gamble?

19. Did you ever have an urge to celebrate any good fortune by a few hours of gambling?

20. Have you ever considered self-destruction or suicide as a result of your gambling?

Most compulsive gamblers will answer yes to at least seven of these questions.

Reprinted with permission from Gamblers Anonymous.

Gam-Anon is a sister organization to Gamblers Anonymous, based in Whitestone, New York, created to help individuals whose lives have been negatively affected by pathological gamblers, such as the family members of compulsive gamblers.

MEDICATIONS MAY HELP PATHOLOGICAL GAMBLERS

Although Gamblers Anonymous support groups and therapy can help many pathological gamblers, some physicians also prescribe medications to treat this psychiatric condition. No medication has been approved by the Food and Drug Administration (FDA) to treat pathological gambling, however, and thus, any medication used for pathological gambling is considered "off-label," although this use is entirely lawful. However, because it is off-label, some insurance companies may refuse to pay for the cost of the medication. It should also be noted that some medications that are used to treat Parkinson's disease have been found to *cause* pathological gambling in individuals who did not have the problem in the past. The solution for these individuals is to reduce the dosage or stop the medication altogether.

Anticonvulsants

Limited studies with **carbamazepine** (Tegretol), an antiseizure medication, have found this medication effective in treating pathological gambling, particularly a study of just one individual with pathological gambling who did well with this medication.[1] However, patients taking this drug must be carefully observed because there are many serious side effects that may occur. (See Table 7.1.)

Antidepressants

Many **antidepressants** have been tested and found not to be efficacious in individuals with pathological gambling. According to Eric Hollander and colleagues in their chapter on pharmacological treatments for pathological gambling, nefazodone (Serzone) has been found effective in reducing gambling urges, as has citalopram (Celexa).[2] However, nefazodone was withdrawn from the market in the United States and Canada because of liver toxicity.

Most studies on the medications have not used a placebo group, so further studies are needed to account for the "placebo effect." This refers to the effect of giving any medication or a sugar pill (placebo) to a group of individuals, who may believe that they are better merely because they have been given these pills.

Hollander et al. reported on one female pathological gambler who responded well to clomipramine (Anafranil), an antidepressant often used to treat obsessive-compulsive disorder (OCD).[3]

Stimulants

Some researchers have used **modafinil (Provigil)**, a medication that is approved for the treatment of narcolepsy, to treat pathological gambling. In one study of 25 females who were pathological gamblers, researchers found distinctive differences in the effects of this medication on gamblers; for example, among the gamblers who were very high in impulsivity, the medication worked well in decreasing the desire to gamble, decreasing the rate of risky decision-making and improving the subjects' ability to inhibit their own behavior. However, among those gamblers rated low in impulsivity, the medication had the opposite effect, increasing the gambling drive.[4]

Since many pathological gamblers are highly impulsive, and some have attention deficit/hyperactivity disorder (ADHD), modafinil may prove to be a helpful medication for the highly impulsive gambler, while it should be avoided in those who are not impulsive or do not have ADHD. However, some insurance companies may refuse to pay for this medication, since it is an off-label use to treat pathological gambling. (As mentioned, all medications for treating gambling are off-label.)

Naltrexone

Research studies have demonstrated the effectiveness of naltrexone in decreasing the gambling urges and behavior of the

Table 7.1 List of Medications to Treat Pathological Gambling: Brand Name,
Generic Name, Type of Medication, and Possible Side Effects*

MEDICATION GENERIC NAME	BRAND NAME	TYPE OF MEDICATION	USUALLY PRESCRIBED FOR	POSSIBLE SIDE EFFECTS*
Naltrexone	ReVia	Opioid antagonist	Alcohol or drug dependence	Nausea, insomnia, headache, anxiety, weight loss, and other adverse effects. Should not be given to patients with liver disease. Liver damage can occur with high dosages. Naltrexone should not be combined with disulfiram because of risk for liver toxicity.
Nalmefene	Revex	Opioid antagonist	Alcohol dependence	Nausea. Does not elevate liver enzymes as does naltrexone.
Disulfiram	Antabuse	Aldehyde dehydro-genase inhibitor	Alcohol dependence	Sedation, fatigue, headaches. Should not be given to patients with liver disease. Severe nausea and vomiting if this drug is combined with alcohol.
Modafinil	Provigil	Stimulant	Narcolepsy; sometimes used off-label for ADHD	Nausea, headache, diarrhea, decreased appetite.

pathological gambler.[5] Naltrexone is a medication that is also used to treat individuals who are dependent on alcohol, and it serves to block or blunt the pleasurable aspects of drinking,

MEDICATION GENERIC NAME	BRAND NAME	TYPE OF MEDICATION	USUALLY PRESCRIBED FOR	POSSIBLE SIDE EFFECTS*
Lithium	No brand name	Mood stabilizer	Bipolar disorder	Gastrointestinal distress, cognitive impairment, tremors, weight gain.
Carbamazepine	Tegretol	Anticonvulsant	Seizure disorders	Nausea, vomiting, loss of appetite, diarrhea, or constipation. Note: Black box warning from the FDA for life-threatening reactions in less than 1% of patients, such as aplastic anemia, thrombocytopenia, and agranulocytosis.
Citalopram	Celexa	Selective sero-tonin reuptake inhibitor (SSRI) antidepressant	Depression	Nausea, diarrhea, decreased appetite, headaches.
Clomipramine	Anafranil	Tricyclic antidepressant	Depression, obsessive-compulsive disorder	Blurred vision, dry mouth, increased sensitivity to sun exposure (heat intolerance).

Note: No medication is approved by the Food and Drug Administration (FDA) to treat pathological gambling and thus all listed medications in the table are "off-label," or legally allowed to be prescribed but not FDA-approved for this treatment.

*Side effects were derived from Lawrence J. Albers, M.D., Rhoda K. Hahn, M.D., and Christopher Reist, M.D. *Handbook of Psychiatric Drugs*. Blue Jay, Calif.: Current Clinical Strategies Publishing, 2008.

much as it does with the pleasure experienced by the pathological gambler in gambling. Studies indicate that a low dose of naltrexone (50 mg per day) has the same level of efficacy as higher doses (100 mg per day or 150 mg per day) in treating pathological gambling.[6]

Nalmefene

Nalmefene (Revex) is a drug similar to naltrexone, which is used to treat individuals addicted to drugs and is sometimes used off-label to treat pathological gambling. According to Jon E. Grant and colleagues, nalmefene may cause nausea but does not have the negative liver effects (hepatotoxicity) that are sometimes associated with naltrexone. It has been proven effective in reducing gambling and even thoughts of gambling.[7]

Lithium

Lithium is a drug that is approved to treat individuals with bipolar disorder, formerly known as manic depression. It is sometimes used to treat pathological gambling and some success has been found.[8] However, lithium is associated with a risk of severe weight gain—up to 100 pounds.[9]

Disulfiram

Some experts have speculated that disulfiram (Antabuse) can be effective in treating pathological gambling as it is in treating alcoholism. Disulfiram is a medication that prevents the body from metabolizing alcohol, and if the individual consumes even a minute amount of alcohol, the body reacts with nausea and vomiting. The key problem with disulfiram is that its severe side effects (extreme vomiting when even a minute amount of alcohol is consumed) also make medication adherence very poor. Not only is disulfiram an aversive treatment, but the drug also decreases dopamine production in the brain, which may be why how and why it acts to reduce addiction, even in those who are not alcoholics.[10]

Combinations of Medications

After trying one medication to treat pathological gambling and receiving a partial response, some physicians may add another medication. Rodrigo Nicolato et al. reported improvement in treating pathological gambling with a combined treatment of lithium and topiramate (an anti-seizure medication).[11]

THERAPY MAY HELP

There are many possible types of therapy to treat pathological gambling, but the key therapies that are used to treat gambling as well as many other problems linked to behavior center on **cognitive-behavioral therapy** and brief interventions as well as combinations of therapies. There is a high dropout rate in therapy and thus the therapy is often adapted to the individual to keep this issue in mind.

Cognitive-Behavioral Therapy

Cognitive-behavioral therapy (CBT) has proven effective in treating many different psychiatric problems, especially when in conjunction with a Twelve Step support group, such as Gamblers Anonymous. The key principles of CBT are that individuals with severe problems hold irrational ideas and beliefs and they also have internal "self-talk" that reinforces the problem behavior, but this self-talk can be changed by the person, with the help of the therapist. The CBT therapist teaches the person how to identify his or her irrational thoughts and actively challenge them. For example, the pathological gambler often erroneously believes that he or she has control over gambling events, and that enacting particular superstitious rituals will cause him or her to win. These gamblers also often believe that after a "losing

Figure 7.1 Twelve-step support groups such as Gamblers Anonymous can help people overcome gambling problems. *(©Alamy)*

streak" they are due for a win, not understanding that each event is independent of the ones before and the ones that follow (in fact, statisticians sometimes call this "gambler's fallacy").

The pathological gambler may believe that he or she needs to win "just one more time," and can then give up gambling. When gambling is pathological, winning is irrelevant and the person will nearly always return to gambling without therapy. A CBT therapist teaches pathological gamblers to challenge their irrational thoughts about gambling.

Brief Interventions

Brief intervention is a process involving one to five sessions designed to make an individual aware of his or her behavior and the likely consequences if this behavior continues. For example, the physician or mental health professional points out to the gambler that the behavior is abnormal and if it continues, his spouse may file for divorce, he may lose his job, and so forth.

Although it might seem on the surface that pathological gamblers already *know* these things, the reality is that often they have convinced themselves that everything is just fine. To hear their own behavior described and the blunt realities of what will happen if it continues can provide sufficient shock to convince some pathological gamblers to change their ways. Reinforcement for the desire to quit gambling can then be provided with a support group, most notably Gamblers Anonymous.

Nancy Petry and colleagues have found that 10 minutes of a brief intervention, which they referred to as "**brief therapy**," was more effective than several sessions of traditional therapy, and

Cognitive Behavioral Therapy and Female Gamblers

In a small study of 19 female pathological gamblers who concentrated on electronic gaming machines, Australian researchers Nicki Dowling and colleagues found that cognitive-behavioral therapy was highly effective and that by the end of the follow-up period of the subjects six months after the therapy, 89% no longer fit the criteria for pathological gambling. The researchers offered 12 sessions.

The first two sessions concentrated on financial limit setting, and the third session centered on alternative activities to gambling. Subsequent sessions covered cognitive correction techniques to gambling and to life in general, problem solving, and communication training. The final two sessions were devoted to relapse prevention.[12]

the researchers found that six weeks later and even nine months later subjects who had a brief intervention had significant reductions in their gambling behavior.[13] With the brief therapy used in this study, the therapist talked about the subject's gambling in relation to gambling by people in the population, described risk factors that led to pathological gambling, and also outlined four steps for an individual to take to cut back on gambling:

- Setting a limit for the amount of money spent on gambling
- Reducing the time spent gambling and the number of days on which he or she gambled
- Ending the view that gambling was a good way to get money
- Spending time on non-gambling activities

According to Damon Lipinski and colleagues, a brief guided self-change (five sessions) approach can be effective with pathological gamblers. Few gamblers seek out therapy, and of those who do, at least half drop out. Lipinski used a five-phase model concentrating on assessment, feedback, **triggers** and consequences, alternatives (to pathological gambling), and relapse prevention. In the assessment stage, the level of gambling is ascertained, and in the feedback stage, the therapist provides feedback on behavior since the first session. With awareness of both triggers to gambling and consequences that result from gambling, the person works on causes and consequences of gambling, such as the need for novelty, competition, and stimulation as well as negative triggers such as fighting with a partner.[14]

The consequences of further gambling are explored, such as financial stress and the loss of respect of others. With the alternatives phase, the person explores alternatives to gambling and identifies high-risk situations for himself or herself, and

Table 7.2: Personalized Feedback Summary

MEASURED GAMBLING BEHAVIOR	TEXT PRESENTED TO CLIENT	QUESTIONS PRESENTED TO CLIENT
Amount intended to gamble over six-month period	Over the course of six months, you gambled 65 times and intended to wager $33,000. This is approximately 46% of your total reported income for this period.	What are some other things that you could have done with your money?
Amount actually wagered over a six-month period	Over the course of six months, you gambled 65 times and actually wagered $68,640. This is approximately 95% of your total reported income for this period. Over the past six months you wagered $35,640 more than you intended. You wagered what you intended on 34 of 65 gambling episodes during the past six months.	Compare the amount you intended to gamble with the money you actually risked gambling. What are your impressions of this comparison?
Time spent gambling over a six-month period	Over the past six months, you have gambled approximately 168 hours, which translated into seven days.	What are some other things that you could have done with that time? Does the amount of time you spent gambling as compared to doing other things reflect your priorities? What's important to you?
Amount won or lost gambling over a six-month period	Your gambling losses for the past 6 months totaled approximately $17,420, which translated into approximately 96% of your total reported income for this period. If you had a job paying just $7 an hour, you would have earned $1,176. Instead, you lost $104 per hour gambling.	You told me about priorities. Does the way you spent money reflect your priorities in life? If someone were to view how you spent your money, would they get an accurate picture of those priorities?
Where does your gambling fit in?	You scored 10 out of possible 20 points on the South Oaks Gambling Screen. A score of 5 or greater is indicative of a potential pathological gambler. A pathological gamer is someone who can experience serious problems from gambling.	About 1% of the adult population scores 5 or above. What do you think about this?

alternative choices that could be made. Last is relapse prevention, in which the person is encouraged to maintain gains and warned about possible relapses as well as future situations that could be high-risk. A personalized feedback summary offered by Lipinski and colleagues is provided in Table 7.2.

Imaginal Desensitization

Another form of therapy that may be effective with pathological gamblers is imaginal desensitization. Often pathological gamblers remember their wins with exquisite clarity while their losses are ignored or buried in their mind. With imaginal desensitization, the therapist teaches individuals to think about their losses and the resulting consequences. In this type of therapy, the individual is desensitized to what they enjoy about gambling and instead is trained to concentrate on the negative consequences caused by pathological gambling.

Adapting Therapy to the Client

Therapists obtain information about the client in the first several sessions. Thus, if the client is largely gambling out of boredom, other, more positive activities that are also exciting can be suggested. In addition, physical exercise can help to increase the level of endorphins (thus increasing a feeling of well-being). However, if the individual is largely gambling to alleviate his or her own stress, as is often true with those who use electronic gaming machines (according to Louise Sharpe), then a better alternative activity would be one that alleviates stress, such as teaching the subject relaxation therapy or yoga training.[15]

A Combination of Therapies

Some researchers have found that a combination of therapies is effective in treating pathological gamblers. For example, Edelgard Wulfert and colleagues reported treating a group of nine severe pathological gamblers with a combination of cognitive behavior therapy and motivational enhancement. They used a combined approach because of the high dropout rate among pathological gamblers. This apparently was the right approach because the gamblers stayed in treatment and for a 12-month follow-up period. Six gamblers maintained complete **abstinence** from gambling, while two improved significantly and one did not improve.[16]

The researchers described Phase 1 of treatment, which used motivation enhancement extended over two or three sessions, with the underlying goals of increasing problem awareness, decreasing client defensiveness and strengthening the commitment to change. The therapist must also obtain information about the particular client and his or her gambling to provide appropriate feedback. The researchers said, "By weighing the negative and positive consequences [of gambling], the client is expected to become more acutely aware of his ambivalence about quitting. Increased awareness together with normative information are hoped to lead to self-motivational statements and the expressed desire to change."[17] Phase 1 ends when the client does commit to comply with the treatment plan.

With Phase 2, the client learns to recognize irrational distortions in his or her thinking as well as triggers that lead to gambling, such as feeling bored, receiving a paycheck, or arguing with a partner or friend. This is also known as cognitive-behavioral therapy. Gamblers are also taught about chance and risks, and that the one thing that can be counted on is that the "house" (those running the gambling operation) wins, and over the short or long term, gamblers always lose. They are also taught the difference between winning in games of chance and winning in games of skill, such as using skill to win at playing chess for money. Many pathological gamblers are drawn to games of pure chance because of irrational views of their own luck or their control over the outcome, and need to learn that their overconfidence ill-serves them and is a factor in their continued gambling.

Noted Edward Gottheil et al., "Problem gamblers also tend to build 'systems' combining spurious environmental signs and complex betting methods to deny the independence of events."[18] This type of thinking is challenged in therapy.

The last phase, Phase 3, covers relapse prevention and shows clients how their thinking and their behavior can lead them to gambling, such as buying a race form, ostensibly just to see who's running today. Coping strategies are also taught, such as learning to deal with overpowering urges to gamble by identifying trigger thoughts and actively disputing them, and using emergency tactics such as leaving the situation or calling a gambling hotline, a friend, or the therapist.

"NATURAL" RECOVERY

It is unknown how frequently it happens, but some pathological gamblers stop gambling on their own, without medication and without therapy. Some researchers refer to this as a "natural" recovery and have sought to analyze those individuals who are more likely to recover in this manner.

For example, in a study by Wendy S. Slutske and colleagues in Australia, the researchers interviewed 104 individuals with a lifetime history of pathological gambling.[19] Of 44 subjects with a past history of pathological gambling but who had exhibited no symptoms in the past 12 months, the researchers found that men were much more likely to recover without treatment than were women, or about 33% of males compared to 38% of female pathological gamblers.

AVOIDING RELAPSES

Many people can stop performing compulsive behaviors—at least for a while. But continuing to avoid pathological gambling can be very difficult, which is why organizations such as Gamblers Anonymous are so important. In addition, it is important for pathological gamblers to identify their own triggers for gambling and develop alternative behaviors, whether a trigger is boredom, a need for stress relief, associating with particular friends, or other triggers. It is sad but true that some friends have a toxic effect on people, and if a particular friend is also a pathological gambler who will encourage someone to gamble, then that friend must be avoided.

In her book on what she calls problem gambling for women (which is apparently pathological gambling by another name), Daine Rae Davis talks about the importance of creating strong barriers that will prevent an individual from relapsing. She offers this example:

> Donna, who knew her own wiliness, put double barriers in place. She not only handed over her checks to someone else, she wrote the check-cashing companies at the casinos and requested they not approve any more of her checks. She also asked them never to change her nonapproval status, even if she made the request. They honored her wishes. Donna knows this because once in the middle of a relapse, she tried to convince them to approve a check. They didn't, and the refusal stopped her relapse. She was able to go home and regroup.[20]

According to Robert Ladouceur and Stella Lachance in their book, *Overcoming Pathological Gambling*, some casinos allow pathological gamblers to self-ban from casinos. Their photo is taken and security guards will stop them if they try to enter the casino. The authors say that this measure can be very effective because it is embarrassing to be publicly banned from a casino, should the individual relapse and try to get into the facility.[21]

If the casino does not have such a program, the pathological gambler can meet the manager of the casino and ask if he or she can be banned from the premises. This will not work all the time, but is one strategy.

The authors offer other helpful suggestions for high-trigger situations. For example, if the person normally drives by the casino after work, he or she must find an alternative route to go home. If the pathological gambler is invited to gamble, say no. Practicing saying no with a therapist can help. Family and friends should also be asked to not invite the person to any place that offers an opportunity to gamble.

It is also important for the pathological gambler to find means to limit his or her access to the money needed to gamble. The pathological gambler can cut up all credit cards and close these accounts. It is also important to avoid carrying an automatic teller machine (ATM) card, which would allow access to the money needed to gamble. This may be inconvenient for those times when a person runs out of cash but for the pathological gambler, it can help to prevent a relapse.

Ladouceur and Lachance also recommend that the pathological gambler who is trying to give up gambling set up an account such that a cosigner is needed for all cash transactions. Friends and family members should be advised to not lend the person any money, no matter how distressed he or she appears and how elaborate and plausible the story he or she weaves. Paychecks should be deposited in the bank directly, rather than given to the person on payday.[22]

Other suggestions offered by Ladouceur and Lachance for recovering pathological gamblers are the following:

- Plan activities so as not to be surprised by the urge to gamble.
- Avoid free time by efficiently managing their use of time.
- Try new and stimulating activities.
- Return to activities they enjoyed before taking up gambling.

- Spend money on other leisure activities.
- Identify concrete goals (short-, mid-, and long-term goals) that they wish to attain.
- Write a motivating sentence on a small card (e.g., "Take care of you," "Do not gamble," "Gambling can only cause problems," "My choice is happiness within my family").[23]

Despite their own best efforts, pathological gamblers may relapse. It is important to avoid common thoughts, such as these:

- I'm hopeless. I can never give up gambling. (Yet the person may not have gambled for a week, a month, or longer, disproving this statement.)
- I am a bad person. (Even good people can relapse. The important thing is to shore up defenses against gambling, rather than wallowing in self-blame, which is more likely to cause further relapses.)
- I am a weak person. (Many people are weak at something, whether it is alcohol, drugs, gambling, chocolate, or another substance or activity. One lapse does not mean that the individual is weak, but rather than he or she is vulnerable.)

David Hodgins and Nancy Petry recommend that the recovering gambler work on planning enjoyable activities ahead of time, especially for high-risk times such as payday or weekends. In addition, they recommend "precommitment activities" such as calling a friend ahead of time to make a date to meet for coffee. Therapists can also help pathological gamblers brainstorm means to handle cravings and unexpected triggers to gambling.[24] Pathological gamblers can recover and this chapter covers the means to recovery, including medication, support groups and therapy.

APPENDIX: SOUTH OAKS GAMBLING SCREEN

Many experts use the South Oaks Gambling Screen to screen subjects for their studies, and this screen is provided below.

1. Please check one answer for each statement:

	Not at all	Less than once a week	Once a week or more
a. Played cards for money.			
b. Bet on horses, dogs, or other animals (at OTB, the track, or with a bookie)			
c. Bet on sports (parlay cards, with bookie, at jai alai).			
d. Played dice games, including craps, over and under, or other dice games			
e. Went to casinos (legal or otherwise)			
f. Played the numbers or bet on lotteries			
g. Played bingo			
h. Played the stock and/or commodities market			
i. Played slot machine, poker machines, or other gambling machines			
j. Bowled, shot pool, played golf, or some other game of skill for money			
k. Played pull-tabs or "paper" games other than lotteries			
l. Played Internet gambling games for money			
m. Some form of gambling not listed above (please specify)			

2. What is the largest amount of money you have ever gambled with on any one day?

___Never gambled   ___More than $100.00 up to $1,000

___$1.00 or less   ___More than $1,000 up to $10,000

___More than $1.00 up to $10.00   ___More than $10,000

___More than $10.00 up to $100.00

3. Do (did) your parents have a gambling problem?

___Both my father and mother gamble (or gambled) too much

___My father gambles (or gambled) too much

___My mother gambles (or gambled) too much

___Neither one gambles (or gambled) too much

4. When you gamble, how often do you go back another day to win back money you lost?

___Never

___Some of the time (less than half the time) I lost

___Most of the time I lost

___Every time I lost

5. Have you ever claimed to be winning money gambling but weren't really? In fact, you lost?

___Never (or never gamble)

___Yes, less than half the time I lost

___Yes, most of the time

6. Do you feel you have ever had a problem with gambling?

___No

___Yes, in the past, but not now

___Yes

7. Did you ever gamble more than you intended to?

___Yes

___No

8. Have people criticized your gambling?

___Yes

___No

9. Have you ever felt guilty about the way you gamble or what happens when you gamble?

___Yes

___No

10. Have you ever felt like you would like to stop gambling but didn't think you could?

___Yes

___No

11. Have you ever hidden betting slips, lottery tickets, gambling money, or other signs of gambling from your spouse, children, or other important people in your life?

___Yes

___No

12. Have you ever argued with people you live with over how you handle money?

___Yes

___No

13. (If you answered yes to question 12): Have money arguments ever centered on your gambling?

___Yes

___No

14. Have you ever borrowed from someone and not paid them back as a result of your gambling?

___Yes

___No

15. Have you ever lost time from work (or school) due to gambling?

___Yes

___No

16. If you borrowed money to gamble or to pay gambling debts, who or where did you borrow from? (Check "yes" or "no" for each.)

	No	Yes
a. From household money		
b. From your spouse		
c. From other relatives or in-laws		
d. From banks, loan companies, or credit unions		
e. From credit cards		
f. From loan sharks ("shylocks")		
g. You cashed in stocks, bonds, or other securities		

	No	Yes
h. You sold personal or family property		
i. You borrowed on your checking account (passed bad checks)		
j. You have (had) a credit line with a bookie		
k. You have (had) a credit line with a casino		

Scores on the South Oaks Gambling Screen itself are determined by adding up the number of questions that show an "at risk" response:

Questions 1, 2, and 3 are not counted. The following questions are counted 1 point each if they are answered as below:

___Question 4: Most of the time I lost, or Every time I lost
___Question 5: Yes, less than half the time I lost, or Yes, most of the time
___Question 6: Yes, in the past, but not now, or Yes
___Question 7: Yes
___Question 8: Yes
___Question 9: Yes
___Question 10: Yes
___Question 11: Yes
Question 12 not counted.
___Question 13: Yes
___Question 14: Yes
___Question 15: Yes
___Question 16a: Yes
___Question 16b: Yes
___Question 16c: Yes
___Question16d: Yes
___Question 16e: Yes
___Question 16f: Yes
___Question 16g: Yes
___Question 16h: Yes
___Question 16i: Yes
Questions 16j and 16k are not counted.

Total = _____ (20 questions are counted)

5 or more points = probable pathological gambler

Source: Henry R. Lesieur, Ph.D. and Sheila B. Blume, M.D., "The South Oaks Gambling Screen (SOGS): A New Instrument for the Identification of Pathological Gamblers," *American Journal of Psychiatry* 144, no. 9 (1987): pp. 1187–1188.

NOTES

Chapter 1

1. American Psychiatric Association, *Diagnostic and Statistical Manual of Mental Disorders.* 4th ed. Text revision. Washington, D.C.: American Psychiatric Association, 2000, p. 674.
2. Henry R. Lesieur, Ph.D., and Sheila B. Blume, M.D., "The South Oaks Gambling Screen (SOGS): A New Instrument for the Identification of Pathological Gamblers," *American Journal of Psychiatry* 144, no. 9 (1987): pp. 1184–1188.
3. Richard C. McCorkle, *Gambling and Crime Among Arrestees: Exploring the Link.* Washington, D.C.: National Institute of Justice, 2004.
4. Ronald C. Kessler, et al., "The Prevalence and Correlates of DSM-IV Pathological Gambling in the National Comorbidity Survey Replication," *Psychological Medicine* 38, no. 9 (2008): pp. 1351–1360.
5. Dean Gerstein, et al., "Gambling Impact and Behavior Study: Report to the National Gambling Impact Study Commission," April 1, 1999. Chicago: National Opinion Research Center at the University of Chicago, 1998. Available online at http://www2.norc.org/new/pdf/gamble.pdf. Accessed February 26, 2010.
6. Kessler, et al., "The Prevalence and Correlates of DSM-IV Pathological Gambling."
7. American Psychiatric Association, *Diagnostic and Statistical Manual of Mental Disorders*, p. 674.
8. Robert H. Pietrzak and Nancy M. Petry, "Severity of Gambling Problems and Psychosocial Functioning in Older Adults," *Journal of Geriatric Psychiatry and Neurology* 19 (2006): pp. 106–113.
9. Renee M. Cunningham-Williams, et al., "Prevalence and Predictors of Pathological Gambling: Results from the St. Louis Personality, Health and Lifestyle (SLPHL) Study," *Journal of Psychiatric Research* 39, no. 4 (2005): pp. 377–390.
10. Gerda Reith, "Gambling and the Contradictions of Consumption: A Genealogy of the 'Pathological' Subject," *American Behavioral Scientist* 51, no. 1 (2007): p. 42.
11. Jeffrey L. Derevensky, Rina Gupta, and Laurie Dickson, "Prevention and Treatment of Adolescent Problem and Pathological Gambling." In Jon E. Grant, J.D., M.D., and Marc N. Potenza, M.D., eds., *Pathological Gambling: A Clinical Guide to Treatment.* Arlington, Va.: American Psychiatric Publishing, 2004, p. 164.
12. Stefano Pallanti, M.D., Nicolo Baldini Rossi, M.D., and Eric Hollander, M.D., "Pathological Gambling." In Eric Hollander, M.D., and Dan J. Stein, M.D., eds., *Clinical Manual of Impulse-Control Disorders.* Arlington, Va.: American Psychiatric Publishing, 2006, pp. 251–289.

Chapter 2

1. Steve Durham and Kathryn Hashimoto, *The History of Gambling in America.* Upper Saddle River, N.J.: Pearson Education, 2010.
2. Durham and Hashimoto, *The History of Gambling in America*, p. 54.
3. Vicki Abt, James F. Smith, and Eugene Martin Christiansen, *The Business of Risk: Commercial Gambling in Mainstream America.* Lawrence: University Press of Kansas, 1985.
4. John M. Findlay, *People of Chance: Gambling in American Society from Jamestown to Las Vegas.* New York: Oxford University Press, 1986.
5. Durham and Hashimoto, *The History of Gambling in America.*

6. Ibid.
7. Abt, Smith, and Christiansen, *The Business of Risk*.
8. Ibid.
9. Findlay, *People of Chance*.
10. Ibid.
11. Durham and Hashimoto, *The History of Gambling in America*, p. 54.
12. Durham and Hashimoto, *The History of Gambling in America*, p. 70.
13. New Hampshire Lottery Commission, "History of the New Hampshire Lottery." Available online at http://www.nhlottery.com/AboutUs/History.aspx. Accessed January 23, 2010.
14. Durham and Hashimoto, *The History of Gambling in America*.
15. Jennifer W. Chiang, "Don't Bet On It: How Complying with Federal Internet Gambling Law Is Not Enough," *Shidler Journal for Law, Commerce + Technology*. June 6, 2007. Available online: http://www.lctjournal.washington.edu/Vol4/a02Chiang.html. Accessed April 13, 2010.
16. Ibid.
17. Ibid.
18. Karen Finlay, et al., "Casino Décor Effects on Gambling Emotions and Intentions." *Environment and Behavior* (August 2009).
19. Ibid.

Chapter 3

1. Renee M. Cunningham-Williams, et al., "Taking Chances: Problem Gamblers and Mental Health Disorders—Results from the St. Louis Epidemiologic Catchment Area Study," *American Journal of Public Health* 88 (1998): pp. 1093–109; Henry R. Lesieur and R.J. Rosenthal, "Pathological Gambling: A Review of the Literature," *Journal of Gambling Studies* 7 (1991): pp. 5–39.
2. Alesia N. Burge, et al., "Age of Gambling Initiation and Severity of Gambling and Health Problems Among Older Adult Problem Gamblers," *Psychiatric Services* 55, no. 12 (2004): pp. 1437–1439.
3. Renee M. Cunningham-Williams, L.B. Cottler, and S.B. Womack, *Pathological Gambling: A Clinical Guide to Treatment*. Arlington, Va.: American Psychiatric Publishing, 2004, pp. 25–36.
4. Kessler, et al., "Prevalence and Correlates of DSM-IV Pathological Gambling."
5. Ibid.
6. Declan T. Barry, et al., "Differences in Characteristics of Asian American and White Problem Gamblers Calling a Gambling Helpline," *CNS Spectrum* 14, no. 2 (2009): pp. 83–91.
7. Rachel A. Volberg and Matt Wray, "Legal Gambling and Problem Gambling as Mechanisms of Social Domination? Some Considerations for Future Research," *American Behavioral Scientist* 51 (2007): pp. 56–85.
8. Gerstein, et al., "Gambling Impact and Behavior Study."
9. Joseph Westermeyer, M.D., et al., "Lifetime Prevalence of Pathological Gambling Among American Indian and Hispanic American Veterans," *American Journal of Public Health* 95, no. 5 (2005): pp. 862–863.
10. Westermeyer, et al., "Lifetime Prevalence of Pathological Gambling," pp. 860–866.
11. Robert T. Wood and Robert J. Williams, "Problem Gambling on the Internet: Implications for Internet Gambling," *New Media & Society* 9, no. 3 (2007): pp. 520–542.
12. Nancy M. Petry, "Internet Gambling: An Emerging Concern in Family

Practice Medicine?" *Family Practice Advance Access* 23 (2006): pp. 421–426.

13. "Online Gambling: A Proposed Licensing Program Would Provide Oversight to Wagering," *Los Anges Times,* August 12, 2010. Available online at http://www.latimes.com/news/opinion/editorials/la-ed-gambling-20100812,0,7035423.story.

14. Cunningham-Williams, et al., "Prevalence and Predictors of Pathological Gambling."

15. Ibid.

16. Ibid.

17. McCorkle, *Gambling and Crime Among Arrestees.*

18. Gerstein, et al., "Gambling Impact and Behavior Study."

19. A. Ibanez, et al., "Gender Differences in Pathological Gambling," *Journal of Clinical Psychiatry* 64, no. 3 (2003): pp. 295–301; Ibanez,. et al., "Gender Differences in Pathological Gambling;" Hermano Tavares, et al., "Factors at Play in Faster Progression for Female Pathological Gamblers," *Journal of Clinical Psychiatry* 64, no. 4 (2003): pp. 433–438.

20. Diane Rae Davis, *Taking Back Your Life: Women and Problem Gambling.* Center City, Minn.: Hazelden, 2009.

21. Silvia Saboia Martins, et al., "Pathological Gambling in Women: A Review," *Revisto dos Hospital das Clínicas* 57, no. 5 (2002): pp. 235–242; McCorkle, *Gambling and Crime Among Arrestees.*

22. Hermano Tavares, et al., "Gender Differences in Gambling Progression," *Journal of Gambling Studies* 17 (2001): pp. 151–159.

23. M.L. Strachan and R.L. Custer, "Female Compulsive Gamblers In Las Vegas." *Gambling Behavior and Problem Gambling* (Reno, NV: Institute for the Study of Gambling and Commercial Gaming, 1993), p. 235–238.

24. Wendy S. Slutske, Alex Blaszczynski, and Nicholas G. Martin, "Sex Differences in the Rates of Recovery, Treatment-Seeking, and Natural Recovery in Pathological Gambling: Results from an Australian Commmunty-Based Twin Survey," *Twin Research and Human Genetics* 12, no. 5 (2009): pp. 425–432.

25. Lynn Blinn-Pike and Sheri Lokken Worthy, "Undergraduate Women Who Have Gambled in Casinos: Are They at Risk?" *Family and Consumer Sciences Research Journal* 37 (2008): pp. 71–83.

26. Jeremiah Weinstock and Nancy M. Petry, "Pathological Gambling College Students' Perceived Social Support," *Journal of College Studies Development* 49, no. 6 (2008): pp. 625–632.

27. Silvia Saboia Martins, et al., "Gender Differences in Mental Health Characteristics and Gambling Among African-American Adolescent Gamblers," *American Journal of Addiction* 1, no. 2 (2008): pp. 126–134.

28. Maggie E. Magoon, Rina Gupta, and Jeffrey Derevensky, "Juvenile Delinquency and Adolescent Gambling: Implications for the Juvenile Justice System," *Criminal Justice and Behavior* 32 (2005): pp. 690–713.

29. Burge, et al., "Age of Gambling Initiation and Severity of Gambling and Health Problems."

30. Frederick W. Preston, Paul D. Shapiro, and Jennifer Reid Keene, "Successful Aging and Gambling:

Predictors of Gambling Risk Among Older Adults in Las Vegas," *American Behavioral Scientist* 51, no. 1 (2007): pp. 102–121.

31. Burge, et al., "Age of Gambling Initiation and Severity of Gambling and Health Problems."

32. Robert H. Pietrzak and Nancy M. Petry, "Severity of Gambling Problems and Psychosocial Functioning in Older Adults," *Journal of Geriatric Psychiatry and Neurology* 19 (2006): pp. 106–113.

33. Jon E. Grant, J.D., M.D., et al., "Late-Onset Pathological Gambling: Clinical Correlates and Gender Differences," *Journal of Psychiatric Research* 43, no. 4 (2009): pp. 380–387.

34. Personal communication with Jon E. Grant, April 17, 2010.

Chapter 4

1. D.E. Comings, "The Molecular Genetics of Pathological Gambling," *CNS Spectrum* 3 (1998): pp. 20–37.

2. Daniela S.S. Lobo and James L. Kennedy, "Genetic Aspects of Pathological Gambling: A Complex Disorder with Shared Genetic Vulnerabilities," *Addiction* 104 (2009): pp. 1454–1465.

3. Louise Sharpe, "A Reformulated Cognitive-Behavioral Model of Problem Gambling: A Biopsychosocial Perspective," *Clinical Psychology Review* 22 (2002): pp. 1–25.

4. National Institute of Mental Health, "The Numbers Count: Mental Disorders in America." Available online: http://www.nimh.nih.gov/health/publications/the-numbers-count-mental-disorders-in-america/

index.shtml#ADHD. Accessed April 18, 2010.

5. Liana Schreiber, et al., "Characteristics of Pathological Gamblers with a Problem Gambling Parent," *American Journal on Addictions* 18, no. 6 (2009): p. 466.

6. Liana Schreiber, et al., "Characteristics of Pathological Gamblers," pp. 462–469.

7. Lobo and Kennedy, "Genetic Aspects of Pathological Gambling," pp. 1454–1465.

8. Sharpe, "A Reformulated Cognitive-Behavioral Model of Problem Gambling."

9. Jon E. Grant, M.D., and Suck Won Kim, M.D., "Medication Management of Pathological Gambling," *Minnesota Medicine* 89, no. 9 (2006): pp. 44–48.

10. Grant and Kim, "Medication Management of Pathological Gambling."

11. Reith, "Gambling and the Contradictions of Consumption;" Damon Lipinski, James P. Whelan, and Andrew W. Meyers, "Treatment of Pathological Gambling Used a Guided Self-Change Approach," *Clinical Case Studies* 6, no. 5 (2007): pp. 394–411; Robert J. Williams, Jennifer Royston, and Brad F. Hagen, "Gambling and Problem Gambling within Forensic Populations: A Review of the Literature," *Criminal Justice and Behavior* 32, no. 6 (2005): pp. 665–689; Sharpe, "A Reformulated Cognitive-Behavioral Model of Problem Gambling;" Howard J. Shaffer and David A Korn, "Gambling and Related Mental Disorders: A Public Health

Analysis," *Annual Review of Public Health* 23 (2002): pp. 171–212.

12. A. Roy, et al., "Pathological Gambling: A Psychobiological Study," *Archives of General Psychiatry* 45 (1988): pp. 369–373.

13. J. Michael Bostwick, M.D., et al., "Frequency of New-Onset Pathologic Compulsive Gambling or Hypersexuality After Drug Treatment of Idiopathic Parkinson's Disease," *Mayo Clinic Proceedings* 84, no. 4 (2009): pp. 310–316.

Chapter 5

1. Kessler, et al., "Prevalence and Correlates of DSM-IV Pathological Gambling."

2. R.C. Bland, et al., "Epidemiology of Pathological Gambling in Edmonton," *Canadian Journal of Psychiatry* 38 (1993): pp. 108–112.

3. Renee Cunningham-Williams, et al., "Problem Gambling and Comorbid Psychiatric and Substance Use Disorders Among Drug Users Recruited from Drug Treatment and Community Settings, *Journal of Gambling Studies* 16 (2000): pp. 347–376.

4. Cunningham-Williams, et al., "Taking Chances."

5. Cunningham-Williams, et al., "Problem Gambling and Comorbid Psychiatric and Substance Use Disorders."

6. Nancy M. Petry, et al., "Comorbidity of DSM-IV Pathological Gambling and Other Psychiatric Disorders: Results from the National Epidemiologic Survey on Alcohol and Related Conditions," *Journal of Clinical Psychiatry* 66 (2005): pp. 564–574.

7. Edward Gottheil, M.D., et al., "Pathologic Gambling: A Nonsubstance, Substance-Related Disorder?" *Journal of Addiction Medicine* 1, no. 2 (2007): pp. 53–61.

8. Cunningham-Williams, et al., "Problem Gambling and Comorbid Psychiatric and Substance Use Disorders."

9. R.A. McCormick, et al., "Affective Disorders Among Pathological Gamblers Seeking Treatment," *American Journal of Psychiatry* 141 (1984): pp. 215–218.

10. Cunningham-Williams, et al., "Taking Chances."

11. Cunningham-Williams, Cottler, and Womack, in *Pathological Gambling*, pp. 25–36.

12. Cunningham-Williams, et al., "Prevalence and Predictors of Pathological Gambling."

13. Cunningham-Williams, et al., "Problem Gambling and Comorbid Psychiatric and Substance Use Disorders."

14. Westermeyer, et al., "Lifetime Prevalence of Pathological Gambling," pp. 860–866.

15. Jessie L. Breyer, et al., "Young Adult Gambling Behaviors and Their Relationship with the Persistence of ADHD," *Journal of Gambling Studies* 25, no. 2 (2009): 227–238.

16. Andrew F. Pasternak IV, M.D., and Michael Fleming, M.D., "Prevalence of Gambling Disorders in Primary Care Setting," *Archives of Family Medicine* 8 (1999): pp. 515–520.

17. Ibid.

18. Benjamin J. Morasco, et al., "Severity of Gambling Is Associated with Physical and Emotional Health in Urban Primary Care Patients,"

General Hospital Psychiatry 28 (2006): pp. 94–100.

19. Morasco, et al., "Severity of Gambling Is Associated with Physical and Emotional Health," p. 99.

Chapter 6

1. Hanne Gro Wenzel, Anita Oren, and Inger Johanne Bakken, "Gambling Problems in the Family—A Stratified Probability Sample Study of Prevalence and Reported Consequences," *BMC Public Health* (2008). Available online at http://www.biomedcentral.com/1471-2458/8/412. Accessed February 4, 2010.
2. Gerstein, et al., "Gambling Impact and Behavior Study."
3. Tracie O. Afifi, et al., "The Relationship of Gambling to Intimate Partner Violence and Child Maltreatment in a Nationally Representative Sample," *Journal of Psychiatric Research* 44, no. 5 (April 2010): pp. 331–337.
4. Attila J. Pulay, M.D., et al., "Violent Behavior and DSM-IV Psychiatric Disorders: Results from the National Epidemiologic Survey on Alcohol and Related Conditions," *Journal of Clinical Psychiatry* 69 no. 1 (2008): pp. 12–22.
5. Jon E. Grant, M.D., and Suck Won Kim, M.D., "Demographic and Clinical Features of 131 Adult Pathological Gamblers," *Journal of Clinical Psychiatry* 2 (2001): pp. 957–962.
6. Jon E. Grant, M.D., et al. "Pathologic Gambling and Bankruptcy," *Comprehensive Psychiatry* 51 (2010): pp. 115–120.
7. Rick Bragg, "End Video Poker Gambling, South Carolina Chief Urges," *New York Times.* January 22, 1998. Available online: http://www.nytimes.com/1998/01/22/us/end-video-poker-gambling-south-carolina-chief-urges.html?pagewanted=1. Accessed March 31, 2010.
8. Williams, Royston, and Hagen, "Gambling and Problem Gambling within Forensic Populations."
9. McCorkle, *Gambling and Crime Among Arrestees.*
10. Ibid.
11. Ibid.
12. Williams, Royston, and Hagen. "Gambling and Problem Gambling within Forensic Populations."
13. Magoon, Gupta, and Derevensky, "Juvenile Delinquency and Adolescent Gambling."

Chapter 7

1. Eric Hollander, M.D., Alicia Kaplan, M.D., and Stefano Pallanti, M.D., "Pharmacological Treatments." In Jon E. Grant, J.D., M.D., and Marc N. Potenza, M.D., eds., *Pathological Gambling: A Clinical Guide to Treatment.* Washington, D.C.: American Psychiatric Publishing, 2004, pp. 189–201.
2. Ibid.
3. Ibid.
4. Martin Zack and C.X. Poulos, "Effects of the Atypical Stimulant Modafinil on a Brief Gambling Episode in Pathological Gamblers with High vs. Low Impulsivity," *Journal of Psychopharmacology* 23, no. 6 (2009): pp. 660–671.
5. Jon E. Grant, et al., "A Double-blind, Placebo-controlled Study of the Opiate Antagonist Naltrexone in the Treatment of Pathological Gambling

Urges," *Journal of Clinical Psychiatry* 69, no. 5 (2008): pp. 783–789.

6. Ibid.

7. Jon E. Grant, et al., "A Multicenter Investigation of the Opioid Antagonist Nalmefene in the Treatment of Pathological Gambling," *American Journal of Psychiatry* 163, no. 12 (2006): pp. 303–312.

8. S. Pallanti et al., "Lithium and Valproate Treatment of Pathological Gambling: A Randomized Single-Blind Study." *Journal of Clinical Psychiatry* 64. 2002 :559–564.

9. Mark S. Gold, M.D. and Christine Adamec, *The Encyclopedia of Alcoholism and Alcohol Abuse* (New York: Facts On File, Inc. 2010).

10. K.S. Barth and R.J. Malcolm, "Disulfiram: An Old Therapeutic with New Applications." *CNS & Neurological Disorders Drug Targets* 9, no. 1 (2010): 5–12.

11. Rodrigo Nicolato, Marco A. Romano-Silva, and Humberto Correa, et al., "Lithium and Topiramate Association in the Treatment of Comorbid Pathological Gambling and Bipolar Disorder," *Australian and New Zealand Journal of Psychiatry* 41, no. 7 (2007): p. 628.

12. Nicki Dowling, David Smith, and Trang Thomas, "Treatment of Female Pathological Gambling: The Efficacy of a Cognitive-Behavioural Approach." *Journal of Gambling Studies* 22, no. 4 (2006): pp. 355–372.

13. Nancy M. Petry, et al., "A Randomized Trial of Brief Interventions for Problem and Pathological Gamblers," *Journal of*

Consulting and Clincal Psychology 76, no. 2 (2008): pp. 318–328.

14. Lipinski, Whelan, and Meyers, "Treatment of Pathological Gambling."

15. Sharpe, "A Reformulated Cognitive-Behavioral Model of Problem Gambling."

16. Edelgard Wulfert, et al., "Retaining Pathological Gamblers in Cognitive Behavior Therapy through Motivational Enhancement: A Pilot Study," *Behavior Modification* 30, no. 3 (2006): pp. 315–340.

17. Edelgard Wulfert, et al., "Retaining Pathological Gamblers in Cognitive Behavior Therapy," p. 325.

18. Gottheil, et al., "Pathologic Gambling: A Nonsubstance, Substance-Related Disorder?" p. 58.

19. Slutske, Blaszczynski, and Martin, "Sex Differences in the Rates of Recovery."

20. Davis, *Taking Back Your Life*, pp. 175–176.

21. Robert Ladouceur and Stella Lachance, *Overcoming Pathological Gambling: Therapist Guide.* New York: Oxford University Press, 2007.

22. Ladouceur and Lachance, *Overcoming Pathological Gambling.*

23. Ladouceur and Lachance, *Overcoming Pathological Gambling,* p. 43.

24. David C. Hodgins and Nancy M. Petry, "Cognitive and Behavioral Treatments." In Jon E. Grant, M.D., J.D., and Marc N. Potenza, M.D., eds., *Pathological Gambling: A Clinical Guide to Treatment.* Washington, D.C.: American Psychiatric Publishing, 2004, pp. 169–187.

abstinence—Refraining altogether from behavior that has been a problem in the past, such as the former pathological gambler refraining from all gambling. Many self-help groups support abstinence, whether the problem behavior is gambling, drinking, or using drugs.

antianxiety medications—Medications used to treat anxiety disorders. The medication used often depends on the type of the anxiety disorder.

antidepressants—Medications used to treat depression, which is a common problem among pathological gamblers.

antisocial personality disorder—A psychiatric disorder that is characterized by the commission of criminal acts and a disregard for the rights of others. Some pathological gamblers have antisocial personality disorder.

anxiety disorders—Serious psychiatric disorders such as specific phobia disorder, generalized anxiety disorder, and post-traumatic stress disorder. Many pathological gamblers have one or more anxiety disorders.

attention deficit/hyperactivity disorder (ADHD)—A disorder characterized by impulsivity and distractibility and sometimes by hyperactivity or inattentiveness. Some individuals with ADHD are pathological gamblers.

bankruptcy—Legal and public declaration of one's inability to pay financial obligations. Bankruptcy is a common problem among pathological gamblers, who spend their money on gambling rather than paying their bills.

brief therapy—Therapy that involves one or several sessions and concentrates on showing the individual the likely consequences of continuing current irrational behavior. Brief therapy has proven successful in some patients.

carbamazepine (Tegretol)—An antiseizure medication that some experts have used off-label and found effective in treating pathological gambling.

casino—A facility that offers gambling and may offer slot machines, card games and other gambling opportunities. Some states allow casinos and Native American reservations may have casinos.

chasing losses—Continuing to gamble despite having recently lost money. This is a characteristic behavior of the pathological gambler, who irrationally believes because that she or he is now "due" for a win. In reality, with games of chance, each event is independent of the one before it.

child abuse—Maltreatment of a child, including physical, emotional or sexual abuse as well as neglect of a child; for example, failing to provide food for an infant or failing to take an ill child to the doctor. Some pathological gamblers are child abusers and/or neglect their children.

cognitive-behavioral therapy (CBT)—A frequently used form of therapy that teaches individuals to challenge their irrational thoughts, replacing them with rational thoughts. Pathological gambling is steeped in irrational thinking.

compulsive gambling—A term used by some experts and by organizations such as Gamblers Anonymous to denote pathological gambling.

continuum theory—The belief that gambling can be viewed on a continuum, with non-gambling at one end, problem gambling further along the continuum, and pathological gambling as the worst aspect of gambling.

depression—A serious psychiatric disorder of unusually low mood and a lack of interest in activities the individual formerly enjoyed. Some depressed individuals are suicidal. Depression is common among pathological gamblers.

disordered gamblers—A term used by some researchers to encompass both pathological gamblers and problem gamblers.

genetic risk—Some individuals have a biological predisposition toward gambling based on their genetic inheritance.

impulse control disorder—A type of disorder that is caused by a lack of control or impulsive behavior. Pathological gambling is an impulse control disorder. Other impulse control disorders are intermittent explosive disorder, kleptomania, pyromania, and trichotillomania.

impulsivity—A trait characterized by making sudden choices based on little thought and without careful consideration. Individuals high in impulsivity may be drawn to gambling.

Internet gambling—Games of chance that are played over the Internet. Some pathological gamblers do their gambling on the Internet.

lottery—A gambling opportunity in which a person buys a ticket or other option and has a very low risk of gaining a high payoff. Many states offer lotteries to finance state projects.

modafinil (Provigil)—A medication for narcolepsy that some experts have used off-label to treat pathological gamblers.

naltrexone—A medication used to treat alcoholism and that some researchers have used off-label to decrease gambling urges.

natural recovery—Recovering from gambling without medications, therapy, or self-help groups. This is a rare and generally unstudied phenomenon, although one study showed that about a third of men and women experience natural recovery from pathological gambling.

neurochemicals—Brain chemicals such as serotonin and dopamine that are released when an individual experiences exciting events. Some researchers believe that pathological gamblers seek the repeated release of neurochemicals.

novelty-seeking temperament—A frequent need to be exposed to new and exciting experiences, and a trait that is predictive for pathological gambling.

Parkinson's disease—A progressively degenerative brain disorder characterized by slowed and uncontrolled movements as well as impaired balance and coordination. Some medications used to treat Parkinson's disease have triggered pathological gambling behavior in some individuals. Lowering the dosage or changing the medication has resolved the problem.

pathological gamblers—Individuals who meet specific criteria for pathological gambling established by the American Psychiatric Association in the *Diagnostic and Statistical Manual*; for example, they may have jeopardized or lost an important relationship or job or may rely on others to help them when they are in dire financial straits because of gambling.

problem gamblers—A term used by some experts to denote people who have gambling issues but which do not rise to the severity of pathological gambling. Some individuals use this term interchangeably with the term pathological gamblers.

relapse—Returning to problematic behavior such as gambling after a time of abstinence. Relapses are common and do not mean that a person cannot recover.

SOGS-Revised Adolescent (SOGS-RA)—A revised screen of the South Oaks Gambling Screen (SOGS), which is used to diagnose adolescents with a pathological gambling problem.

South Oaks Gambling Screen—A popular screening tool used by many experts to determine if a person is a pathological gambler.

substance abuse or dependence—Excessive use or addiction to alcohol and/or drugs. Many pathological gamblers have substance abuse or dependence issues.

triggers—Events that instigate pathological gambling, such as associating with friends who gamble or experiencing a stressful event. There are many possible triggers, and individuals need to learn what triggers their problem behavior to better combat it.

violence—Physical assault of another adult or child. Some pathological gamblers exhibit violence in their relationships with others.

Books

Abt, Vicki, James F. Smith and Eugene Martin Christiansen. *The Business of Risk: Commercial Gambling in Mainstream America.* Lawrence: University Press of Kansas, 1985.

Davis, Diane Rae. *Taking Back Your Life: Women and Problem Gambling.* Center City, Minn.: Hazelden, 2009.

Durham, Steve and Kathryn Hashimoto. *The History of Gambling in America.* Upper Saddle River, N.J.: Pearson Education Inc., 2010.

Findlay, John M. *People of Chance: Gambling in American Society from Jamestown to Las Vegas.* New York: Oxford University Press, 1986.

Grant, Jon E. *Impulse Control Disorders: A Clinician's Guide to Understanding and Treating Behavioral Addictions.* New York: W.W. Norton, 2008.

Hollander, Eric, and Daniel. J. Stein, eds. *Clinical Manual of Impulse Control Disorders.* Arlington, Va.: American Psychiatric Publishing, 2006.

Ladouceur, Robert, and Stella Lachance, *Overcoming Pathological Gambling: Therapist Guide.* New York: Oxford University Press, 2007.

McCorkle, Richard C. *Gambling and Crime Among Arrestees: Exploring the Link.* Washington, D.C.: National Institute of Justice, 2004.

Web Sites

American Counseling Association

http://www.counseling.org

American Mental Health Counselors Association

http://www.amhca.org

American Psychiatric Association

http://www.psych.org

American Psychological Association

http://www.apa.org

Gam-Anon

www.gam-anon.org

Gamblers Anonymous

www.gamblersanonymous.org

National Alliance on Mental Illness

http://www.nami.org

National Council on Problem Gambling

www.ncpgambling.org

National Mental Health Consumer's Self-Help Clearinghouse

http://www.mhselfhelp.org

Substance Abuse & Mental Health Services Administration

http://www.samhsa.gov

abstinence, 83, 100
Abt, Vicki, 12, 13
accessibility, 32, 86
addiction model, 49–50
ADHD. *See* attention deficit/hyperactivity disorder
adolescent gamblers
 characteristics, 35–39
 incarcerated, 65, 68
 lifelong gambling, 22
 thought processes, 9
adrenaline rush, 8, 50–51
African American gamblers, 23, 29, 36–38
age groups, 26
age of onset, 34, 38–44
aging, ix
alcohol abuse
 in Asian-Americans, 23
 family history of, 43, 47
 linked to pathological gambling,
  52–54, *54*
Alcoholics Anonymous, 69
American Indian military veterans, 26
American Psychiatric Association (APA),
 2, 4
amphetamine dependence, 54
Anafranil, 75
Antabuse, 74, 76
antianxiety medications, 100
anticonvulsants, 72
antidepressants, 72–73, 100
antisocial personality disorder (ASPD),
 56–57, 100
anxiety disorders, 43, 52–53, 55–56, 100
APA. *See* American Psychiatric Association
Asian-American gamblers, 23, 29
ASPD (antisocial personality disorder),
 56–57, 100
Atlantic City, New Jersey, 15–16
attention deficit/hyperactivity disorder
 (ADHD), 46, 52, 57, 73, 100

backache, 57
bankruptcy, 41, 61, 63–64, 100
Barry, Declan T., 23
behavioral addiction, 50

bingo, 18, 33, *33*
Blinn-Pike, Lynn, 35
borrowing money, 1, 24, 27, 86
brain neurochemicals, vi–x, 45, 50–51, 102
brief therapy, 78–82, 100
Burge, Alesia N., 38

Canadian Gambling Index (CGI), 28
carbamazepine (Tegretol), 72, 75, 100
card "sharps," 12
Casino.org, 19
Casino Reinvestment Development
 Authority, 16–17
casinos, *5*
 access to, 32
 Atlantic City, New Jersey, 15–16
 defined, 100
 design of, 20
 female gamblers, 35
 Internet, 19–20
 Las Vegas, Nevada, 14–15
 Native American, 17–19, *18*, 36, 37
 research information, 20–21
 riverboat gambling, 12–13, 36
 self-banning, 85
 types of gambling, 8
causes of pathological gambling, 45–51
 addiction model, 49–50
 brain neurochemicals, 50–51
 continuum theory, 50
 environmental or genetic influences,
  46–49
 genetic risks, 45–46
 Parkinson's disease, 51
CBT (cognitive-behavioral therapy), 77–78,
 101
Celexa, 75
CGI (Canadian Gambling Index), 28
chasing losses, 10, 22, 31, 100–101
Chiang, Jennifer, 19–20
child abuse, 59, 62, 63, 101
childhood experiences, viii–ix, 48–49
child neglect, 49
citalopram (Celexa), 75
clomipramine (Anafranil), 75
cluttered areas, 20–21

cocaine dependence, 54
cognitive-behavioral therapy (CBT), 77–78, 83, 101
colonial era, 11–12
combat status, 28
combined medications, 77
combined therapies, 82–84
Comings, D. E., 45
comorbidity, 62
compulsive gambling, 2, 4–5, 66–67, 70–71, 101
concerned significant others (CSOs), 60–61
Congress, U.S., 15, 19, 30–31
continuum theory, 50, 101
cravings, 50
crime, 34, 64–65, 68
crime syndicates, 14–15
criteria, 2–4
CSOs (concerned significant others), 60–61
Cuba, 14
Cunningham-Williams, Renee M., 5, 23, 29–32, 55
Custer, Robert, 34

Davis, Diane Rae, 33, 85
Department of Justice, U.S., 64–65
depression, 40, 55, 63, 101
Derevensky, Jeffrey, 9
desensitization, 82
Diagnostic and Statistical Manual (DSM), 1, 3, 4
disabled gamblers, 28, 58
disordered gamblers, 5, 101
disulfiram (Antabuse), 74, 76
divorces, 2, 14
dopamine, 45, 50, 51, 76
Dowling, Nicki, 79
drug abuse, 53
DSM. *See Diagnostic and Statistical Manual*
Durham, Steve, 15–16

early-life gambling, 40, 41, 44
education, *25*, 26
elderly gamblers, 38–44
electronic gambling machines, 49
environmental influences, vi–ix, 46–49

euphoria, 8–10, 50
excitement, 8–10, 49

families, 23, 59–64
family history, 43
feedback, 80, 81, 83
female gamblers
    characteristics of, 32–35
    genetic factors, 46
    high information load, 21
    incarcerated, 32, 64
    low income, 24
    parents of, 47
    relapse, 85
    treatment, 79, 84
financial hardship, 62–64
Finlay, Karen, 20–21
the Flamingo casino, 14–15
flashing lights, 20
Fleming, Michael F., 57
Food and Drug Administration, 72
Foxwoods casino, 17

Gam-Anon, 64, 66–67, 72
Gamblers Anonymous, 64, 69–72, 77, 79, 85
gambling
    history of, 11–21
    types of, 6, 8, 42, 49
gender differences, 34–35, 38
genetic influences, vi–viii, 46–49
genetic risk, 45–46, 101
Gottheil, Edward, 53, 84
Grant, Jon E., 49, 50, 62, 76
Great Depression, 13

Hashimoto, Kathryn, 15–16
health issues. *See* psychiatric and health issues
heartburn, 57
heredity, 47
higher-income gamblers, 24, *25*, 27
high information load, 20–21
Hispanic-American military veterans, 26
history of gambling, 11–21
    casino research information, 20–21

ABOUT THE AUTHOR

Christine Adamec is a professional writer who has authored and coauthored more than thirty books on a broad array of topics, including such diverse subjects as drug abuse, attention-deficit/hyperactivity disorder, fibromyalgia, impulse control disorders and adoption. Her most recent books are *The Encyclopedia of Alcohol Abuse and Alcoholism* (Facts On File, 2010) and *The Encyclopedia of Digestion and Digestive Disorders* (Facts On File, 2011).